Teaching Mathematics with Virtual Manipulatives

GRADES K–8

Patricia S. Moyer-Packenham

Didax

Order Number 211047
ISBN 978-1-58324-318-3

A B C D E 14 13 12 11 10

395 Main Street
Rowley, MA 01969
www.didax.com

Contents

Foreword

*A*fter our first applets appeared in 1997, I frequently found myself challenged when offering up the proverbial 30-second elevator definition of virtual manipulatives. I usually muddled about how virtual manipulatives were something like concrete manipulatives that you could move around on the computer screen but could not touch. I knew at the time that this analogy captured only a small part of the power and versatility of virtual manipulatives. While the explanation usually worked with teachers familiar with manipulatives, it almost never worked with the students for whom we developed these tools. When working with students, it seemed more appropriate to point at the website and let them figure it out. New technologies are inherently interesting to students, and these software programs could stimulate learning for weeks.

Patricia Moyer-Packenham and her colleagues defined a virtual manipulative as an "interactive, Web-based, visual representation of a dynamic object that provides opportunities for constructing mathematical knowledge" (Moyer, P., Bolyard, J., and Spikell, M. 2002. What are virtual manipulatives? *Teaching Children Mathematics,* 8 (6): 372–77). For us, this definition captures the essence of what we seek to do: create interactive, dynamic resources that enable learners to "figure it out."

These days, I rarely have to describe virtual manipulatives to teachers. More teachers have grown up with these programs, they have fun using them, and they see utility and purpose in learning activities. I still get the opportunity, once in a while, to practice the elevator spiel with my university colleagues. It was during one of those moments when an esteemed colleague questioned whether anything was lost when young children manipulate a virtual object instead of a physical object. Perhaps I have missed something, but research continues to suggest there is nothing lost by manipulating virtual objects, and there is much to be gained.

To some, the idea of freely available, virtual objects or tools that provide similar and expanded learning opportunities may require a bit of a conceptual shift. However, it is becoming increasingly clear that young school-age children who benefit from modeling using concrete manipulatives also benefit greatly from using virtual manipulatives. With continued use of touch-screen and other emerging technologies, discussions around distinguishing between virtual and concrete will hopefully evolve into how to use what we have to sustain excitement about learning mathematics.

While students seemingly have little trouble with the concept or use of virtual manipulatives, there is the challenge that goes along with any technology that has been around for a while—that of getting beyond ho-hum. What used to stimulate learning and interest for several days can now become passé after a few hours. As is the case with most learning technologies, the challenge for parents and teachers is to learn how to use these tools in ways that promote thinking and enable communication and representation. In order to get past ho-hum, we need to ask good questions and pose problems that challenge our students.

This book is full of ideas that promote that kind of thinking by asking good questions and posing interesting problems that can be explored and solved using virtual manipulatives. Patricia Moyer-Packenham and her colleagues have been studying the use of virtual tools for a long time. They know what works and have put this resource together with the knowledge that these ideas will excite young learners into deeper understanding of mathematics. We welcome the development and sharing of activities that promote thinking!

Jim Dorward, for Bob Heal, Larry Cannon, and Joel Duffin
National Library of Virtual Manipulatives

Acknowledgments

The authors gratefully acknowledge Christopher Johnston (George Mason University), Gwenanne Salkind (George Mason University), and Arla Westenskow (Utah State University) for their invaluable help in reviewing the entire book before publication.

Chapter 1

What Are Virtual Manipulatives?

*I*nnovations in technology, ubiquitous access to the Internet, and the usability of toolkits for creating dynamic computer objects have increased the availability of computer-generated representations for teaching and learning mathematics (Spicer 2000). One result of these advances is an exciting new technology for teaching mathematics called *virtual manipulatives*. Moyer, Bolyard, and Spikell (2002) define a virtual manipulative as "an interactive, Web-based, visual representation of a dynamic object that provides opportunities for constructing mathematical knowledge." Unlike static visual representations, which are essentially pictures on the computer, virtual manipulatives are dynamic and flexible. These objects can be moved, rotated, flipped, and turned, and some can even be changed entirely. (See Figure 1.)

Unique Features and Capabilities of Virtual Manipulatives

Several general features have been identified that make virtual manipulatives uniquely suited for mathematics teaching and learning in school environments (Dorward and Heal 1999; Moyer, Niezgoda, and Stanley 2005). The development of the National Library of Virtual Manipulatives (NLVM) (http://nlvm.usu.edu/en/nav/vlibrary.html), National Council of Teachers of Mathematics (NCTM) *Illuminations* (http://illuminations.nctm.org/Default.aspx), and Shodor Curriculum Materials (http://shodor.com/curriculum/) has

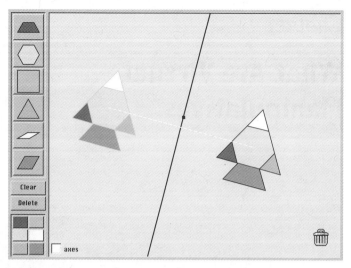

FIGURE 1 *NLVM applet Transformations – Reflections*
© 1999–2008 Utah State University

provided classroom teachers with a wealth of resources linked with national mathematics standards (Cannon, Heal, and Wellman 2000; Dorward and Heal 1999). With a connection to the Internet, virtual manipulatives are free of charge with *anytime access and availability*. Other benefits of virtual manipulatives are their *potential for alteration*, which allows users to mark, color, highlight, or even reconfigure parts of the virtual object, or to input a sequence of numbers or commands to create one's own mathematical problem or simulate a sequence of events. Users can manipulate objects in ways that the objects cannot be manipulated in the physical environment. The *interactivity* of virtual manipulatives enables the user to have input into the actions on the screen and lets the user get information and guidance from the text and images on the screen. Virtual manipulatives link *symbolic and iconic notations* by saving numerical information or providing mathematical notations that label the on-screen objects. (See Figure 2.) In addition, the click of a mouse can provide access to *unlimited materials* and users simply click on-screen icons for *easy clean-up*.

Many of the virtual manipulatives currently available today were designed based on physical manipulatives that are commercially available for mathematics instruction, such as pattern blocks, tangrams, or geometric shapes and solids. Other virtual manipulatives were developed in the electronic environment with no physical counterpart. Whether based on a physical manipulative or developed in the computer environment, the flexibility of virtual manipulatives makes them uniquely suited for teaching mathematics.

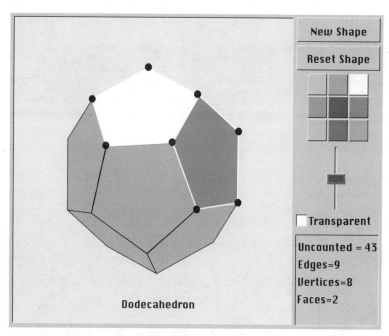

FIGURE 2 *NLVM applet Platonic Solids*
© 1999–2008 Utah State University

Even the virtual manipulatives that are based on physical manipulatives have their own unique qualities. For example, a virtual geoboard models the physical geoboard because users can place the bands on the pegs of the board to create geometric shapes. A unique capability in the virtual environment, however, is that the bands placed on the pegs can be stretched and shaped beyond what is possible in the physical environment, and the areas created by the bands can be colored using a paint palette to highlight portions of the geoboard, portions of the shapes created by the bands, and overlapping portions of the shapes. (See Figure 3.) These images can then be saved and printed from the computer screen so that the user's work on the geoboard is not lost (Clements and Saramas 2002).

Variety among the Virtual Manipulatives Available

There are many variations of virtual manipulatives available for users. Some virtual manipulatives allow more *open-ended explorations* for users while others provide a *guided concept tutorial*. Those that allow more open-ended explorations can be classified

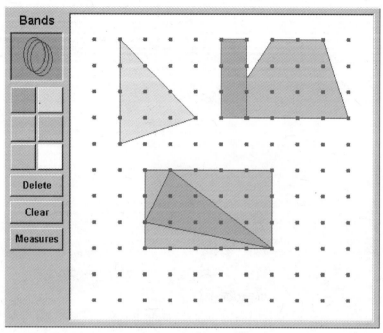

FIGURE 3 *NLVM applet Geoboard*
© 1999–2008 Utah State University

in three groups: *pictorial only, simulation*, and *combined pictorial and numeric*.

- *Pictorial-only* virtual manipulatives applets feature a visual image of the object with no additional information on the screen. For example, pattern blocks are an example of this type of applet. (See Figure 4.)
- *Simulations* allow users to run trials that repeat multiple actions on the screen for the user. For example, a student can use a simulation numbers board (or hundreds board) to find the Sieve of Eratosthenes by selecting and running repeated multiples until the numbers board displays all of the prime numbers.
- *Combined pictorial and numeric* applets provide a visual image with accompanying numeric displays that correspond to manipulations of the electronic objects. An example of this is the base-10 blocks applet that displays ones, tens, and hundreds blocks along with a corresponding number sentence for students to solve.

The virtual manipulatives that provide a *guided concept tutorial* have multiple features for interaction with the user. An exam-

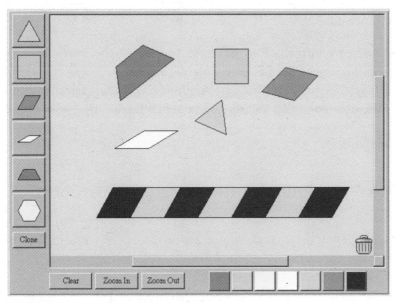

FIGURE 4 *NLVM applet Pattern Blocks*
© 1999–2008 Utah State University

ple of this type of applet would be a fraction addition applet where portions of regions are shaded and a number sentence requires the user to add two fraction amounts with unlike denominators. The following attributes are included in the concept tutorial:

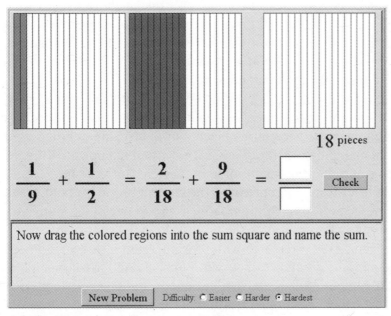

$$\frac{1}{9} + \frac{1}{2} = \frac{2}{18} + \frac{9}{18} = \boxed{}$$ 18 pieces

Now drag the colored regions into the sum square and name the sum.

New Problem   Difficulty: ○ Easier ○ Harder ◉ Hardest

FIGURE 5 *NLVM applet Fractions – Adding*
© 1999–2008 Utah State University

- Directions that verbally guide the user through the steps to solving the exercise
- Numeric information that corresponds to the user's actions on the objects in the tutorial environment
- Text that provides guiding feedback and correction to help the user compute the on-screen algorithm

(See Figure 5.)

Virtual Manipulative Research in Classrooms

Research on virtual manipulatives is in its early stages, but there is promising evidence that the unique affordances of virtual manipulatives can have positive effects on student learning.

Comparison Studies Using Physical and Virtual Manipulatives

Some of the first research studies on virtual manipulatives have compared them to physical manipulatives to determine whether they are equally effective. Among the studies comparing physical and virtual manipulatives are Suh (2005) and Suh and Moyer-Packenham's (2007) comparisons of two groups of third graders placed in physical and virtual manipulative treatment groups to study algebra and rational number concepts. While students performed equally well when solving algebraic equations, there were significant differences in favor of the virtual manipulatives when students learned addition of fractions with unlike denominators. The findings indicated unique characteristics in the design of the virtual fraction applet that influenced student achievement.

Steen, Brooks, and Lyon (2006) randomly assigned 31 first-grade students to treatment and control groups, where both groups studied the same geometric objects, but the treatment group used virtual manipulatives for practice. The virtual manipulatives treatment group showed significant improvements on first- and second-grade level tests, and outscored the control group on both grade level tests, even though the treatment group began the study at a significantly lower level on the pretests than the control group.

Kim's (1993) research with 35 kindergarten students showed no significant differences between physical and virtual manipulative treatment groups studying arithmetic and geometry concepts. However, there were other features in the virtual manipulatives environment that appealed to teachers and students. Similarly, Martin and Lukong (2005) found that both physical and virtual manipulatives were equally effective with 31 randomly assigned first-grade students when solving measurement division problems. Additionally, Terry's (1996) study of 102 students in grades 2 through 5 demonstrated that there were significant pre- to post-test gains when students used both physical *and* virtual manipulatives, rather than the physical or the virtual manipulatives *alone*.

Takahashi's (2002) research focused on the unique affordances in both environments. This study of two sixth-grade classes using virtual and physical geoboards revealed that the physical geoboard might be a more appropriate tool for use in a lesson focused on developing the concept of area, while the virtual geoboard might be a more appropriate tool for a lesson focused on the transformation of shapes to develop one's own formula for area. These results highlight the importance of considering the unique features of virtual environments and ways those features can enhance mathematical learning, rather than on choosing between physical and virtual manipulatives.

Studies Examining Unique Capabilities

Some of the research on virtual manipulatives focuses on identifying unique characteristics and affordances provided in the virtual environment. For example, Reimer and Moyer (2005) studied 19 third-grade students who used several virtual fraction applets in a computer lab during a two-week unit on rational numbers. In addition to a statistically significant improvement in students' post-test scores on a test of conceptual knowledge, student interviews and attitude surveys indicated that the virtual manipulatives: a) helped students learn more about fractions by providing immediate and specific feedback, b) were easier and faster to use than paper-and-pencil methods, and c) enhanced students' enjoyment while learning mathematics. In research on fifth-graders of different achievement levels, Suh, Moyer, and Heo (2005) found that the concept tutorials supported students' learning of equivalence and fraction addition in the following ways: a) allowed discovery learning through experimentation and hypothesis testing, b) encouraged students to see mathematical relationships, c) connected iconic and symbolic modes of representation explicitly, and d) prevented common error patterns in fraction addition. Similarly, Suh and Moyer (2007) found that virtual manipulatives enhanced third-grade students' ability to flexibly translate their understanding across representations including: manipulative models, pictorial images, numeric information, and word problems.

Moyer, Niezgoda, and Stanley's (2005) research in kindergarten and second-grade classrooms examined how the tools themselves can influence the way that young children communicate their mathematical thinking. In this study, kindergarten children used virtual pattern blocks, wooden pattern blocks, and drawings on three different days. When using the virtual pattern blocks, children made a greater number of patterns, used more elements in their pattern stems, and exhibited more creative pattern behaviors. In the second-grade classroom examined in this research, students used virtual base-10 blocks to add whole numbers (Moyer, Niezgoda, and Stanley, 2005). An assessment of students, which required them to write, draw, and compute sums of whole numbers, showed that the virtual base-10 blocks provided a visual model that students used when representing the addition exercises on the assessment. Similarly, Bolyard's (2006) examination of two different virtual manipulative applets for teaching the same concepts in integer addition and subtraction showed that the applets provided a visual model that aided students in creating their own representations to solve problems on the assessment. In other studies, the unique capabilities of virtual manipulatives have been shown to positively influence students' time-on-task (Drickey 2000) and improve students' confidence in mathematics (Heo, Suh, and Moyer 2004).

While many studies focus on the benefits of virtual manipulatives, researchers caution teachers to use virtual manipulatives selectively. Although Izydorczak (2003) found some favorable characteristics of virtual manipulatives, her research also notes the rote use of virtual manipulatives, the need for teacher direction and guidance when using virtual manipulatives, design features of the virtual manipulatives that are not used to their full potential resulting in representations that are not linked, difficulty with user controls, and information that could cause distraction for users. Similarly, Brown (2004) reported on the considerations necessary for the use of virtual manipulatives in classrooms, including motivation, unique instructional capabilities, instructional support, required skills, and teacher productivity.

Publications Featuring Virtual Manipulative Lessons

More recent research has examined the frequency with which teachers are beginning to integrate virtual manipulatives as instructional tools and ways teachers are using virtual manipulatives in their lessons. In a study of 95 lessons, Moyer, Salkind, and Bolyard (2008) found that the most frequent content areas where virtual manipulatives were used included *numbers and operations* and *geometry*; that virtual geoboards, pattern blocks, tangrams, and base-10 blocks were the virtual manipulatives most commonly used; and that virtual manipulatives were often used by teachers in combination with physical manipulatives.

In other publications, researchers and teachers have developed lessons for the use of virtual manipulatives in K–12 mathematics teaching. For example, Beck and Huse (2007) describe a probability lesson where students run simulations using the virtual coin toss and the virtual spinner. In *Teaching Children Mathematics,* Moyer-Packenham (2005) published a lesson that provides directions for third- through fifth-grade students to investigate algebra concepts through numerical patterns and shape patterns using a virtual calculator, virtual hundreds board, and virtual pattern blocks. In this investigation, students create patterns, recognize and verbally describe pattern relationships, generalize rules about those pattern relationships, and represent them with tables.

Bolyard and Moyer (2003) have created lesson ideas for exploring the concept of function in algebra in grades 6 through 8 by using virtual pattern blocks, a virtual graphing tool, and a spreadsheet. The use of virtual manipulatives for these lessons allows students to generate and compare various representations of a function and enables them to focus on the mathematics of the tasks by eliminating the distraction of tedious computations. In another lesson for middle school students, the authors use virtual pattern blocks, platonic solids, and geoboards to describe three investigations for promoting geometric thinking by allowing students to experiment with the virtual manipulative to represent abstract concepts (Moyer and Bolyard 2002). These published lessons provide teachers with guidance on how to use virtual manipulatives effectively for mathematics instruction.

Summary

Although research on virtual manipulatives is still in its early stages, there is much that can be learned about their use from these initial classroom studies and sample lessons. A variety of unique characteristics make virtual manipulatives well-suited for use in school mathematics teaching. One appeal of virtual manipulatives in mathematics teaching environments is that their capabilities often go beyond the capabilities of physical manipulatives. There is also evidence that virtual manipulatives are as useful as physical manipulatives for student achievement, and in some cases have unique affordances that enhance students' learning and ability to communicate mathematical ideas. A small collection of ideas for their use in classroom lessons is growing. This text adds to this foundation by providing educators with direction on the selection of virtual manipulatives for mathematical tasks, how to use virtual manipulatives in assessment, and technical guidance to enhance usability for classroom teachers. Our goal is to support the use and usefulness of these dynamic tools for school mathematics instruction.

References

Beck, S. A., and V. E. Huse. 2007. A virtual spin on the teaching of probability. *Teaching Children Mathematics* 13(9): 482–486.

Bolyard, J. J. 2006. *A comparison of the impact of two virtual manipulatives on student achievement and conceptual understanding of integer addition and subtraction.* Unpublished doctoral dissertation, George Mason University, Fairfax, Virginia.

Bolyard, J. J., and P. S. Moyer. 2003. Investigations in algebra with virtual manipulatives. *ON-Math, Online Journal of School Mathematics* 2(2): 1–10.

Brown, E. R. 2004. Virtual manipulatives in the classroom: What considerations are necessary? *Society for Information Technology and Teacher Education International Conference* 2004(1): 4378–4381.

Cannon, L. O., E. R. Heal, and R. Wellman. 2000. Serendipity in interactive mathematics: Virtual (electronic) manipulatives for learning elementary mathematics. *Journal of Technology and Teacher Education, Proceedings of the Society for Information Technology & Teacher Education*, San Diego, California, February 2000.

Clements, D. H., and J. Saramas. 2002. The role of technology in early childhood learning. *Teaching Children Mathematics* 8(6): 340–343.

Dorward, J., and R. Heal. 1999. National library of virtual manipulatives for elementary and middle level mathematics. *Proceedings of WebNet 99 World Conference on the WWW and Internet*, Honolulu, Hawaii, October 1999. Association for the Advancement of Computing in Education, 1510–1512.

Drickey, N. A. 2000. A comparison of virtual and physical manipulatives in teaching visualization and special reasoning to middle school mathematics students. *Dissertation Abstracts International* 62(02A): 499.

Heo, H.-J., J. Suh, and P. S. Moyer. 2004. Impacting student confidence: The effects of using virtual manipulatives and increasing fraction understanding. *The Journal of Educational Research in Mathematics* 14(2): 207–219.

Izydorczak, A. E. 2003. *A study of virtual manipulatives for elementary mathematics.* Unpublished doctoral dissertation, State University of New York at Buffalo.

Kim, S.-Y. 1993. The relative effectiveness of hands-on and computer-simulated manipulatives in teaching seriation, classification, geometric, and arithmetic concepts to kindergarten children. *Dissertation Abstracts International* 54(09A): 3319.

Martin, T., and A. Lukong. 2005. *Virtual Manipulatives: How effective are they and why?* American Educational Research Association Annual Conference, Montreal, Canada.

Moyer, P. S., and J. J. Bolyard. 2002. Exploring representation in the middle grades: Investigations in geometry with virtual manipulatives. *The Australian Mathematics Teacher* 58(1): 19–25.

Moyer, P., J. Bolyard, and M. Spikell. 2002. What are virtual manipulatives? *Teaching Children Mathematics* 8 (6): 372–377.

Moyer, P. S., D. Niezgoda, and J. Stanley. 2005. Young children's use of virtual manipulatives and other forms of mathematical representations. In W. J. Masalski and P. C. Elliott (Eds.), *Technology-supported mathematics learning environments: Sixty-seventh yearbook* (pp. 17–34). Reston, VA: NCTM.

Moyer, P. S., G. Salkind, and J. J. Bolyard. 2008. Virtual manipulatives used by K-8 teachers for mathematics instruction: Considering mathematical, cognitive, and pedagogical fidelity. *Contemporary Issues in Technology and Teacher Education* 8(3): 1–17.

Moyer-Packenham, P. S. 2005. Using virtual manipulatives to investigate patterns and generate rules in algebra. *Teaching Children Mathematics* 11(8): 437–444.

Reimer, K., and P. S. Moyer. 2005. Third graders learn about fractions using virtual manipulatives: A classroom study. *Journal of Computers in Mathematics and Science Teaching* 24(1): 5–25

Spicer, J. 2000. Virtual manipulatives: A new tool for hands-on math. *ENC Focus* 7(4): 14–15.

Steen, K., D. Brooks, and T. Lyon. 2006. The impact of virtual manipulatives on first grade geometry instruction and learning. *Journal of Computers in Mathematics and Science Teaching* 25(4): 373–391.

Suh, J. M. 2005. *Third graders' mathematics achievement and representation preference using virtual and physical manipulatives for adding fractions and balancing equations.* Unpublished doctoral dissertation, George Mason University, Fairfax, Virginia.

Suh, J., and P. S. Moyer. 2007. Developing students' representational fluency using virtual and physical algebra balances. *Journal of Computers in Mathematics and Science Teaching* 26(2): 155–173.

Suh, J. M., and P. S. Moyer-Packenham. 2007. The application of dual coding theory in multi-representational virtual mathematics environments. In J. H. Woo, H. C. Lew, K. S. Park, and D. Y. Seo (Eds.), *Proceedings of the 31st conference of the International Group for the Psychology of Mathematics Education* (Vol. 4, pp. 209–216).

Suh, J., P. Moyer, and H. J. Heo. 2005. Examining technology uses in the classroom: Developing fraction sense using virtual manipulative concept tutorials. *The Journal of Interactive Online Learning* 3(4): 1–22.

Takahashi, A. 2002. Affordances of computer-based and physical geoboards in problem-solving activities in the middle grades. *Doctoral dissertation, University of Illinois at Urbana-Champaign*, 63(11): 38–88.

Terry, M. K. 1996. An investigation of differences in cognition when utilizing math manipulatives and math manipulative software. *Dissertation Abstracts International*, 56(07A): 2650.

Chapter 2

Selecting Virtual Manipulatives for Classroom Use

*M*s. Smith's third-grade class has been exploring equivalent fractions. The children have examined fractional amounts represented by shading a portion of a rectangular region drawn on grid paper and have found different names for the region by dividing the area into smaller parts. Ms. Smith wants her students to look for patterns in the fraction names they find in order to help them discover a computational procedure for finding equivalent fractions. Today, the students are working with a virtual manipulative tool designed to help them create equivalent fractions. Students are shown a fractional amount represented by the shaded region of a rectangle and the name for that amount. The instructions ask the students to divide the rectangle into different numbers of pieces in order to find equivalent fractions. Once they find a fraction name, they can enter it into the computer and check their answer. Ms. Smith has asked them to record the picture of the original fraction, the name of the original fraction, and any equivalent fractions they find.

One of the third-graders begins with the fraction $\frac{5}{6}$. He begins to manipulate the computer applet to divide the region into more pieces. (See Figure 1.) As he increases the number of divisions, black lines appear on the rectangle, reflecting the new divisions. When the student gets to 12 pieces, the black lines turn red as they match up exactly to the lines demarcating the shaded region. He has found an equivalent fraction. He counts the number of shaded pieces and enters $\frac{10}{12}$ into the computer. The computer tells him that he is correct; $\frac{10}{12}$ is another name for $\frac{5}{6}$. The student records this on his sheet and goes back to work. In a short time, he has found sev-

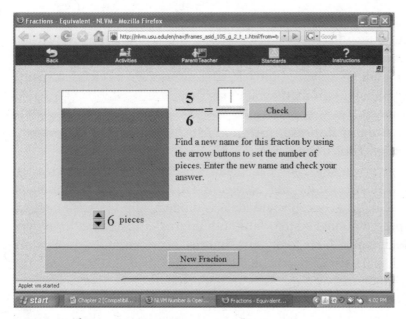

FIGURE 1 *NLVM applet Fractions – Equivalent*
© 1999–2008 Utah State University

eral other names for the region. As he begins to examine his recordings, he believes he has discovered a pattern in the numbers. When he presents his conjecture to Ms. Smith, she suggests that he test his ideas on the next fraction. The virtual manipulative will help him verify his thinking.

What ideas is this student exploring with this virtual manipulative? What features of the virtual manipulative might support his exploration? How did Ms. Smith decide which virtual manipulative to use for this task? How might her choice impact the learning that takes place? These are the questions that will be addressed in this chapter.

How Do Virtual Manipulatives Support Learning?

As described in Chapter 1, a virtual manipulative is "an interactive, Web-based, visual representation of a dynamic object that provides opportunities for constructing mathematical knowledge" (Moyer, Bolyard, and Spikell 2002, 373). How might virtual manipulatives support the construction of new knowledge and what features of these tools might impact learning? Research and theories of learning in the areas of cognitive science, multimedia learning, and the use of representation and technology in mathematics education contribute ideas for consideration. The sections below provide general background information on these ideas and then suggest guidelines based on these ideas to use when selecting virtual manipulatives for mathematics instruction.

The Role of Representation in Mathematics and Learning through Multimedia

As stated in the National Council of Teachers of Mathematics' (NCTM) *Principles and Standards* (2000), the representation of mathematical concepts and ideas is fundamental to understanding. Representational systems are both internal and external in nature (Goldin and Shteingold 2001). Internal representation systems are those that exist within the mind of the individual, that is, the way the individual makes sense, sees, or understands ideas. External representations can be used to communicate an individual's mathematical ideas and understandings to others. This may be done through multiple representational forms, including manipulative models, pictures, written symbols, real-world situations, and oral language (Lesh, Post, and Behr 1987). Each of these forms has the potential to highlight different features of a mathematical idea or relationship (NCTM 2000). Translating among and between these representational forms builds understanding of mathematical ideas (Hiebert 1990).

Research on multimedia learning and instructional design provides theoretical models for understanding how the use of different representational forms may impact learning. Multimedia is generally defined as combining words (including written and spoken) and pictures (including static or dynamic objects and graphs) in an instructional presentation (Reed 2006). Learning theories from the field of cognitive science have influenced research in multimedia learning through three basic ideas: (1) humans process information through two channels, visual-pictorial and auditory-verbal; (2) these channels can hold and process a limited amount of knowledge at a given time; and (3) learning occurs as pieces of information in the channels interact and integrate with each other and with prior knowledge (Mayer 2002). These three assumptions have informed several principles in the design of multimedia learning instruction with the goal of better learning and retention (Mayer 2002). The main principle states that it is better to present an explanation in words and pictures than solely in words. The presentation should locate related words and pictures near each other, should present words and pictures simultaneously, and should eliminate extraneous words, pictures, and sounds. The presentation should provide signals for key ideas or steps and should allow the user some control over the words, pictures, and pace of the presentation. This interaction may reduce the cognitive load on working memory, enabling the user to pause, organize, and reflect on new information, allowing for building a mental model (Mayer and Chandler 2001).

The Use of Technology to Support Mathematics Learning

Although the multimedia principles discussed above apply to instruction across all types of media (text, illustrations, etc.), there are unique features of some media that may allow instructional design opportunities that are not readily available in other forms. Technology is one example. According to NCTM (2000), the use of technology in mathematics teaching and learning is essential due to its capabilities to (a) produce detailed visual images of mathematics concepts, (b) facilitate the organization and analysis of data, and (c) support the investigation of new concepts and ideas. Technology makes it possible for virtual and other computer-based manipulative programs to build in instructional supports that must otherwise be incorporated into instruction from an outside source. Such features include multiple, linked representations, interactivity, and immediate feedback.

Virtual manipulatives are examples of *externalized representations* (Zbiek, Heid, Blume, and Dick 2007) through which students can communicate their internal representations of mathematical ideas. They can act as a visual model of a mathematical process or idea (Kurz, Middleton, and Yanik 2005). In addition, virtual manipulatives are *cognitive technical tools* (Zbiek, Heid, Blume, and Dick 2007) which enable users to perform an action on a representation of a mathematical object or concept and see the result of that action. In the example described at the beginning of the chapter, the student clicked on a command to increase the number of divisions in the rectangular region. As he did, he could see the area being divided into increasingly smaller pieces. If he instructed the computer to lower the number of divisions, the pieces would become fewer and larger. The tool served as a visual model of the relationship between the number of pieces into which a whole is divided and the size of those pieces.

Furthermore, unlike other external representations, these computerized versions have the ability to link multiple representational forms of mathematical concepts in dynamic ways so that action on one form (such as a manipulative or object) is reflected not just in that form, but in other forms as well (for example, the symbolic notation). These links help students see connections among representations of a concept, while highlighting the unique features of the concept evident in each representational form.

Technology tools, like virtual manipulatives, also provide constraints that highlight or signal important ideas to ensure that students are engaging with the relevant mathematics. For example, the tool used in Ms. Smith's classroom provided a pictorial representation that illustrated when the number of divisions created by the student aligned with the original amount. Originally, the lines bounding the fractional region were red. As the additional divisions are created, the lines representing them are black. Once an equivalent amount is found, all lines turn red, signaling that an equivalent fraction has been found.

Constraints and other features available in technology environments can support actions on objects that are more closely representative of the mathematical relationship being explored than can other types of medium (such as physical tools) (Zbiek, Heid, Blume, and Dick 2007). For example, if students were exploring equivalent fractions on paper and creating the divisions by hand, it might be expected that they would have difficulty accurately dividing the region into equivalent and increasingly smaller pieces. It is likely that students would find one or two equivalent amounts and then be stalled due to the difficulty of creating accurate divisions. Using the virtual tool, the students can create divisions up to 99 pieces. This more closely represents the behavior of rational numbers in the sense that the same number can be expressed in infinite ways.

Finally, virtual manipulatives support the exploration of rich mathematical ideas, such as pursuing hypotheses. In the case of the equivalent fraction tool, the student felt he had discovered a pattern in the equivalent fraction names. Rather than having to repeatedly draw new fractions and create multiple divisions by hand, the student could use the virtual tool to assist him in these processes. The capabilities of the computer to accurately and efficiently create new divisions and provide feedback on the accuracy of his entries removed these responsibilities from the student and allowed him to focus on testing and refining his emerging ideas.

How to Select a Virtual Manipulative

Virtual manipulatives can represent mathematical ideas while incorporating multimedia design principles and taking advantage of the supports and features made possible through technology. Considering the potential of these tools, how does one select a virtual manipulative for classroom use? The next section provides some suggestions, guidelines, and questions to consider in this process.

Guidelines for Selecting a Virtual Manipulative

1. The first and most important consideration is, what is the mathematics that you wish to teach? While this may seem obvious, clearly defining your goals and objectives is the first and most important step in selecting a virtual manipulative or any other instructional tool. Is your mathematical goal conceptual (i.e., developing an understanding of equivalent fractions, or understanding the relationship between the number of parts in a whole and the size of the parts)? Is your goal to develop or practice a skill (i.e., developing a computational procedure for finding equivalent fractions)? Being clear about the purpose of the lesson or unit will help you determine the most effective instructional approach.

2. Once you have determined your instructional goals and objectives, ask yourself, is a virtual manipulative an appropriate way to reach these goals? What can the virtual manipulative add to instruction that might not be available or possible in another medium? Can it extend the mathematical possibilities that could be explored beyond what is possible using another tool? Would the use of a combination of virtual and physical manipulatives enhance students' experiences? Identifying the unique features of a virtual manipulative that could enhance and support student learning will help you create instructional experiences that will utilize these features more effectively.

3. Is the virtual manipulative an appropriate mathematical model for the concept or skill you want the user to explore? Does the model have the potential to accurately represent the user's developing understanding of mathematical ideas? Will the actions performed with the virtual manipulative appropriately reflect the mathematical ideas being explored? In other words, how well does the behavior of the virtual manipulative reflect the ideas the task is designed to address?

4. Is the virtual manipulative applet interactive? Are images dynamic and interesting (but not too "busy")? What is required of the user? Can users control on-screen objects and representations or are they simply observing actions on the screen? Are the user's actions accurately reflected in the tool? Are

they allowed control over the pace of the exploration or task to allow time for mental processing?

5. Does the website include multiple representations of the concept? Are words, numerals, and pictures on the site used simultaneously to connect representations? Are these representations linked so that the user's actions on one representation are reflected in other representational forms?

6. What type of feedback does the site provide? Is constructive feedback provided? Are correct responses confirmed? Are incorrect responses signaled? If so, how? The type of feedback desired may vary with your goal. For example, if the goal is to practice or develop a specific procedure, feedback that guides the learner through each step would be appropriate. If the goal is to provide students opportunities to develop concepts or test conjectures, more open-ended feedback may be more appropriate.

7. What constraints, supports, or scaffolding does the site provide? Are there constraints that may help students focus on the relevant mathematical ideas? Are there constraints built in that highlight ideas and that may not be available in another medium? Are there hints or suggestions that will help students continue to work on the ideas if they get stuck? Is there a way to make modifications or accommodations in order to meet the needs of diverse learners?

8. Is the site user friendly, with clear instructions for manipulating dynamic features? Would students be able to engage with the site on their own, or would you need to provide instruction for your students? If so, what kind of instruction would be most effective?

9. Other considerations: Can the tools on the site can be altered and used to teach several different concepts (when appropriate)? How can you record or keep a record of what students have done? Are there activities, lessons, or other teacher resources available?

The questions in the above list may be numerous, but they are not intended to form an exhaustive list. Rather, they are offered as suggestions for consideration. It may be unlikely that any tool, virtual manipulative or otherwise, will have all of the features suggested above. However, with an understanding of how these tools may support learning to guide your selection, you, as the teacher, can better determine which features might be most important for the learning goal and your students.

References

Goldin, G., and N. Shteingold. 2001. Systems of representations and the development of mathematical concepts. In A. A. Cuoco and F. R. Curcio (Eds.), *The roles of representation in school mathematics: NCTM yearbook 2001* (pp. 1–23). Reston, VA: NCTM.

Hiebert, J. 1990. The role of routine procedures in the development of mathematical competence. In T. J. Cooney and C. R. Hirsch (Eds.), *Teaching and learning mathematics in the 1990s: NCTM yearbook 1990* (pp. 31–40). Reston, VA: NCTM.

Kurz, T. L., J. A. Middleton, and H. B. Yanik. 2005. A taxonomy of software for mathematics instruction. *Contemporary issues in technology and teacher education* [Online serial] 5(2). Retrieved June 12, 2008, from http://www.citejournal.org/vol5/iss2/mathematics/article1.cfm.

Lesh, R., T. Post, and M. Behr. 1987. Representations and translations among representations in mathematics learning and problem solving. In C. Janvier (Ed.), *Problems of representation in the teaching and learning of mathematics* (pp. 33–40). Hillsdale, NJ: Erlbaum.

Mayer, R. E. 2002. Cognitive theory and the design of multimedia instruction: An example of the two-way street between cognition and instruction. *New Directions for Teaching and Learning* 89: 55–71.

Mayer, R. E., and P. Chandler. 2001. When learning is just a click away: Does simple user interaction foster deeper understanding of multimedia messages? *Journal of Educational Psychology* 24: 390–397.

Moyer, P. S., J. J. Bolyard, and M. A. Spikell. 2002. What are virtual manipulatives? *Teaching Children Mathematics* 8: 372–377.

National Council of Teachers of Mathematics. 2000. *Principles and standards for school mathematics*. Reston, VA: Author.

Reed, S. K. 2006. Cognitive architectures for multimedia learning. *Educational Psychologist* 41: 87–98.

Zbiek, R. M., M. K. Heid, G. W. Blume, and T. P. Dick. 2007. Research on technology in mathematics education: The perspective of constructs. In F. Lester (Ed.), *Handbook of research on mathematics teaching and learning* (pp. 1169–1207). Charlotte, NC: Information Age Publishing.

Chapter 3

Using the Unique Features of Virtual Manipulatives to Design Lessons

When designing lessons using virtual manipulatives, teachers need to understand what it means to use technology "appropriately" to teach mathematics. The five guidelines for appropriate uses of technology specific to mathematics education are

1. Introduce technology in context
2. Address worthwhile mathematics with appropriate pedagogy
3. Take advantage of technology
4. Connect mathematics topics
5. Incorporate multiple representations (Garofalo et al., 2000, p. 67)

In addition to knowing how to integrate technology appropriately, teachers must focus on worthwhile mathematics and effective pedagogy when using technology. One effective way to do this is to plan mathematics tasks focused on the five process standards (NCTM 2000): representations, communications, connections, reasoning and proof, and problem solving. This chapter focuses on incorporating the guidelines for appropriate uses of technology specific to mathematics and optimizing learning environments with virtual manipulatives and applets.

The template in Figure 1 may be used during planning to guide the activity and classroom discussion so they focus on advancing students' mathematical thinking.

Website	http://nlvm.usu.edu/en/nav/frames_asid_172_a_2_t_3.html?open=activities&from=category_a_2_t_3.html

Math Strand	Geometry	Grade level 2–5	
Description of mathematical concept (NCTM/SOL)	Properties of plane shapes Area and perimeter of polygons Symmetry and congruence		

Analysis of Mathematical Representations and Models

__Concept tutorial/skill practice __ Investigation/problem solving __Open exploration

Mathematical thinking opportunities afforded by the mathematics applet

Representations: • Create and use representations to organize, record, and communicate mathematical ideas • Use mathematical representations to solve problems • Use representations to model and interpret physical, social, and mathematical ideas	Explain: This virtual geoboard is versatile in that it can model multiple polygons, line segments, and angles, build symmetrical and congruent shapes and be used to find area and perimeter. The screen includes the visual (virtual geoboard) and the numeric (measures).
Communication: • Use the language of mathematics to express mathematical ideas precisely	Explain: Students could construct figures based on descriptions given, or give descriptions of their own shapes for a partner to build. Given names of shapes, students could construct them and then compare. The geoboard offers a great way to develop vocabulary and language.
Connections: • Provides connections among mathematical ideas • Relates how mathematical ideas interconnect and build on one another to produce a coherent whole • Applies mathematics in contexts outside of mathematics	Explain: The connection between the created shapes and the perimeter and area through the Measure button allows for students to relate to the meaning of the two forms of measurement concepts. This easily connects to the development of fractions.
Reasoning and Proof: • Develops reasoning and proof • Opportunities to investigate mathematical conjectures	Explain: Students could explain how the formulas for area and perimeter work for different polygons.
Problem Solving: • Opportunities to apply and adapt a variety of appropriate strategies to solve problems	Explain: Students can click on the Activities button to solve a variety of problems. Students could use different ways to find the area of irregular polygons.

FIGURE I *Example of the "Advancing Mathematical Thinking" planning sheet*

Exploring Relationships among Equivalent Fractions (Fourth-Grade Lesson)

The following sections describe how technology was used to teach a mathematics lesson. We describe the task and the tool that supported the learning, the role of the teacher in capitalizing on the learning in the technology-rich environment, and how the technology gave more access and opportunity to diverse learners for learning. The planning sheet presented in Figure 1 was used to think through the instructional elements in the design of the lesson.

The Mathematical Task and the Technology Tools as Learning Supports

In the fourth-grade lesson on fractions, the objective was to rename fractions and find equivalent fractions using the virtual manipulative called Fraction Equivalence found at the National Library of Virtual Manipulatives (NLVM) (http://nlvm.usu.edu/en/nav/vlibrary.html). (See Figure 2.) The lesson was designed to let students explore the relationships among equivalent fractions by analyzing patterns in a list of equivalent fractions. The goal was to help students generalize rational number concepts based on the pattern they identified among the fractions and then construct a rule for themselves.

During the task, students were presented with a fraction circle or square with parts shaded and were directed, "Find a new name for this fraction by using the arrow buttons to set the number of pieces. Enter the new name and check your answer" (as shown in Figure 2). To find the new fraction name, students clicked on arrow buttons below the whole unit, which changed the number of parts. When students had an equivalent fraction, all lines turned red. When a common denominator was identified, students typed in the number for each equivalent fraction in the appropriate box. Students checked their answers by clicking the Check button. Once they were given feedback, they were asked to find several other names for that fraction. Each step of the way, the pictures were linked to numeric symbols that dynamically changed with moves made by the students. To help students explore the relationships among equivalent fractions, the applet prompted students to find several equivalent fractions. This applet was specifically designed to develop the concept of renaming fractions. Although constrained to one specific objective, the tool allowed for more exploration than do physical manipulatives, such as fraction circles or bars, which are usually limited by the number of fractional pieces. This applet

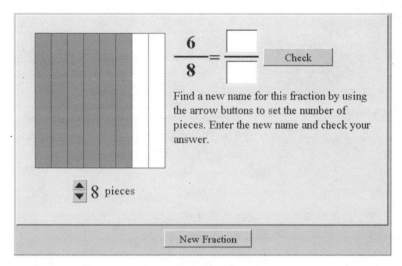

FIGURE 2 *NLVM applet Fractions – Equivalent*
© 1999–2008 Utah State University

enabled students to equally divide a whole into 99 pieces, which allowed them to generate multiple equivalent fraction names.

In addition to many of the design features that enhance student learning, each applet has language options for Spanish, French, and English. This particular classroom was in a Title I school that was predominately Hispanic, and the opportunity to select the Spanish language option was a great learning support for students (see Figure 3).

The Role of the Teacher in Facilitating Learning in a Technology-Rich Environment

The teacher's role in extending students' thinking during this task was to encourage students to record a list of equivalent fractions, and then to determine patterns among the numbers to eventually generate a rule. For example, using the applet on a SMART Board, one student demonstrated $\frac{1}{3} = \frac{2}{6} = \frac{3}{9} = \frac{4}{12}$. As the class recorded this on the board, students' eyes widened and hands went up in the air, with students saying, "Oh, oh, I know the rule!" When students shared their rules, some noticed the additive rule. One student stated, "The denominators are going by a plus 3 pattern." Another student shared, "It's like skip counting." Another voiced, "It's the multiple of 3." To encourage their understanding of the mathematical relationships, the teacher asked students to explore the fraction $\frac{2}{3}$ so that they could see the multiplicative pattern for the numerator and the denominator. For example, students listed $\frac{2}{3} = \frac{4}{6} = \frac{6}{9}$, and

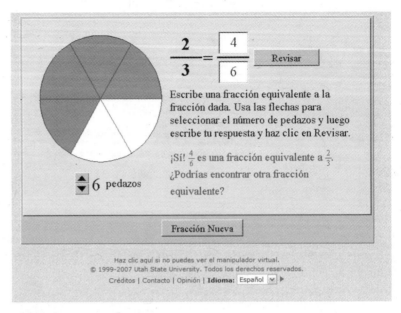

FIGURE 3 *NLVM appletFractions – Equivalent in Spanish*
© 1999–2008 Utah State University

again they quickly saw the additive pattern and the multiples of 2 for the numerator and 3 for the denominator.

Next the teacher posed questions to extend their investigation: "Are $\frac{2}{3}$ and $\frac{20}{30}$ equivalent fractions? What about $\frac{2}{3}$ and $\frac{10}{15}$?" Students used the applet and talked with a partner to identify relationships between the given fractions and to explore other fractions to find a rule beyond the additive rule.

When students gathered again as a group, several students shared their discoveries. One student noted, "The fractions $\frac{2}{3}$ and $\frac{20}{30}$ are equivalent because you multiply both numerator and denominator by 10. And in $\frac{2}{3} = \frac{10}{15}$, you multiply both numerator and denominator by 5." This discussion led to a lively conversation on how $\frac{10}{10}$ is one whole and $\frac{5}{5}$ is one whole. The teacher connected this idea to the identity property of multiplication by asking, "What happens when we multiply 1 by any number?" This discussion reinforced the idea that no matter how you rename the fractions, as long as you multiply it by 1 or $\frac{n}{n}$, you will have an equivalent fraction.

To challenge the students, the teacher posed a new question: "What would the equivalent fraction be for $\frac{1}{3}$ if the denominator was divided into 99 parts?" This type of questioning encouraged students to extend their thinking by making conjectures and testing their rule or hypothesis.

A critical part of lesson planning is making sure there is time for mathematical discourse before, during, and after using the technology tool. As students explore patterns and relationships, it is critical that they participate in mathematical discourse with their peers and their teacher.

Opportunities to Learn via Technology: Equity and Access for Diverse Learners

Using the Fraction applet helped students think and reason about the relationships among equivalent fractions, instead of merely mimicking an algorithm demonstrated by the teacher. In this class, the teacher matched student partners so that a student with limited proficiency in English was paired with a student who spoke both English and Spanish proficiently. As the pairs worked together with the applet, they were able to make sense of the mathematics by talking through the processes. In addition, the ability to switch the language to Spanish gave many of the English language learners access to the mathematics, as shown in Figure 3.

Learners with special needs, including language needs, are often given direct instruction on how to perform an algorithm us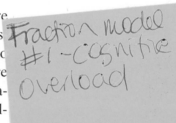ing mnemonic devices or steps to follow without an opportunity to construct a conceptual understanding of the procedures they are performing. One challenge when students work with physical manipulatives, such as fractions circles, is that the manipulation of multiple pieces creates too much of a cognitive load on students' thinking processes and students lose sight of the mathematics concept. In this classroom example, when students worked with the virtual applet, the applet off-loaded some of the physical manipulation so that students could focus more on the mathematical processes and the relationships among the equivalent fractions. An additional support for special needs students was provided by the instructor, who worked with a small group of students on the SMART Board while the other students explored at individual computers with their partners.

Overall, this applet gave students with special needs access to the mathematics without creating a cognitive overload. Having the visual and numeric representations closely tied together and displayed on the screen helped students make direct connections in the relationships among equivalent fractions. Throughout the lesson the teacher worked with a small group of English language learners and special needs students on the SMART Board. These students required more teacher support and benefited from the small group interaction. Also, the kinesthetic/tactile advantages of the SMART Board enabled these students a greater understanding of the concept. The teacher was able to reteach and reinforce skills as needed. Students took turns manipulating the SMART Board and guiding each other through the given task.

Leveraging Technology to Enhance the Mathematical Learning

Learning environments that take advantage of virtual manipulatives offer a number of affordances for students as they develop their mathematical understanding. The example presented in this chapter identifies five primary benefits of virtual manipulatives:

1. Linked representations, providing connections and visualization between numeric and visual representations
2. Immediate feedback, which allows students to check their understanding throughout the learning process and prevents misconceptions
3. Interactive and dynamic objects that take mathematics from a noun to a verb (from *mathematics* to *mathematize*)
4. Opportunities to teach and represent mathematical ideas in nontraditional ways
5. Ease of differentiation and scaffolding to meet the needs of diverse learners

Recording Students' Mathematical Thinking and Learning

As teachers structure their learning environments using technology, the primary focus should be on supporting mathematical understanding. There are a number of design and assessment issues that are unique to using technology. For example, teachers should consider having students use a task sheet to record their work and thoughts, and asking students to record examples from the virtual manipulative by printing their work. By writing and recording their work, students can reflect on their own experiences, a metacognitive process that is essential in problem solving. The task sheet (like the one shown in Figure 4) can facilitate this recording process and provides a permanent record, which can be used for assessment purposes by the teacher.

Appropriate use of technology in teaching and learning should make the learning environment qualitatively different than teaching without it. That is, integration of technology should not merely add a virtual representation to the lesson but should enhance the mathematics teaching and learning by providing opportunities for

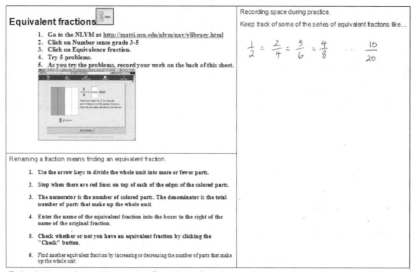

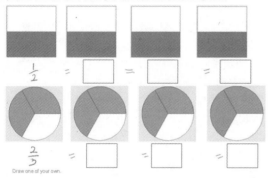

Find equivalent fractions for these fractions. Draw what each fraction looks like on the screen.

Can you make a rule for finding equivalent fractions? Does it work for every fraction? Test out your rule with some other fractions. Prove your thinking.

FIGURE 4   *Tasksheet to record students' thinking while using the tool*

rich mathematical thinking and discussion. This means that there are specific pedagogical considerations for teachers. The classroom example illustrates how using the NCTM process standards along with the unique affordances of the technology tools allows for meaningful learning to take place while meeting the needs of diverse learners.

References

Garofalo, J., H. Drier, S. Harper, M. A. Timmerman, and T. Shockey. 2000. Promoting appropriate uses of technology in mathematics teacher preparation. *Contemporary Issues in Technology and Technology Education* 1(1): 66–88.

National Council of Teachers of Mathematics. 2000. Principles and standards for school mathematics. Reston, VA: Author.

Chapter 4

Assessment and Virtual Manipulatives

Assessment of learning comes in two basic forms: formative and summative. *Formative assessment* refers to assessment that helps a teacher discover what students already know and where they are developmentally in order to inform instruction. *Summative assessment* examines what students learned from instruction—it's a summary of what students learned during a given period. There are implications for virtual manipulatives in both forms of assessment.

The National Council of Teachers of Mathematics (NCTM) has published several handbooks describing assessment types and ways to use them in the classroom, including portfolios, teacher notes, tests, and quizzes (e.g., Bush and Greer 1999). The National Library of Virtual Manipulatives (NLVM) has options for collecting results from students' work with virtual manipulatives that can be used to inform instruction and help teachers track progress (http://enlvm.usu.edu). The activities available for students and teachers are wide-ranging, from complex problem-solving activities to tutorials. However, most teachers will probably also need paper-based assessments. Classroom-based assessment is, ultimately, the decision of the teacher.

Adding Fractions

One example of a virtual manipulative that can serve a variety of assessment purposes is the Adding Fractions (Two-Step Sum) applet. Students are given two rational numbers and their representation on a rectangle or a circle. The first step is to rewrite each frac-

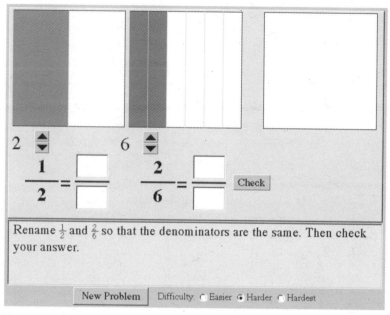

FIGURE 1 *Step 1 of NLVM applet Fractions – Adding*
© 1999–2008 Utah State University

tion with the necessary common denominator. The applet tells the student whether the denominator is correct. To find the denominator, students can change the number of divisions in the shape. (See Figure 1.) When students have selected the correct denominator, the applet divides a rectangle or a circle into the correct number of divisions and students can move the pieces from the previous two shapes over (as illustrated in Figure 2). Then the student selects the correct sum of the two fractions. The applet tells the student whether the answer is correct. Students can select easier, harder, or hardest problems to vary the level of difficulty. The Adding Fractions applet will be used as an example throughout this chapter.

Assessment Framework

Wiliam (2008, 1054) describes an assessment framework that classifies the roles assessment plays in the mathematics classroom to motivate student learning individually and in groups. Table 1 shows how that framework has been mapped onto settings using the Adding Fractions manipulative. Assessment is not separate from classroom activity; rather, activities designed for students' learning are also assessments of their learning. Virtual manipulatives incorporate this idea by being both a means for student learning and a

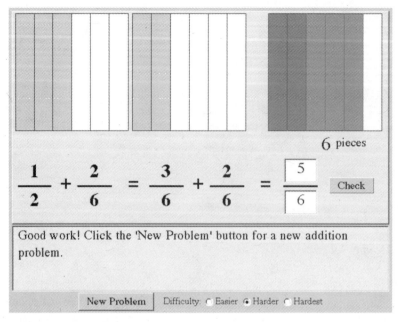

$$\frac{1}{2} + \frac{2}{6} = \frac{3}{6} + \frac{2}{6} = \frac{5}{6}$$

6 pieces

Check

Good work! Click the 'New Problem' button for a new addition problem.

New Problem   Difficulty: ○ Easier ◉ Harder ○ Hardest

FIGURE 2 *Step 2 of NLVM applet Fractions – Adding*
© 1999–2008 Utah State University

means for assessing student learning as the students work through problems using the manipulatives.

Formative Assessment

Since virtual manipulatives are conducive to individualized instruction where students work independently, they can be used to assess what it is students know and are able to do at an individual level. In addition, students' use of the online materials can be easily tailored to their level of learning. Formative assessment outside the virtual manipulative environment can be used to aid teachers' selection of virtual manipulatives for a class or for individual students. Formative assessment has been found to improve student performance (Black, Harrison, Lee, Marshall, and Wiliam 2003). The goal is that students should receive feedback about their progress and the assessment should inform instruction. Formative assessment, in some cases, can be like a dialogue between teacher and student. It is usually more informal (i.e., not a test) and very low-stakes for the student. For example, the student can keep track of how many fraction addition problems were completed to help the teacher measure progress through a lesson. The student could also attempt different levels of difficulty with the fraction addition manipulative.

TABLE 1 Assessment Framework

Item from Wiliam's Framework	Example Using Virtual Manipulatives
Clarifying and sharing learning intentions and criteria for success	Students complete a given number of problems, moving from easier to more difficult addition of fractions problems.
Engineering effective classroom discussion, question and learning tasks that elicit evidence of student learning	Students share the results of their explorations with fractions with the class (e.g., did they notice that there are multiple common denominators?).
Providing feedback that moves learners forward	Applet tells the student at each step of the addition problem whether the answer so far is correct (e.g., correct denominator selected, fractions added correctly).
Activating students as instructional resources for one another	Students can share their work on the manipulative and work together on addition problems.
Activating students as the owners of their own learning	Students can work independently on the manipulative. The teacher can give instruction as to problem level (easy, harder, or hardest).

Virtual manipulatives afford students and teachers the opportunity to tailor instruction to individual needs and pacing. Virtual manipulatives themselves can be used as a formative assessment task to document student knowledge. By analyzing students' responses on individual tasks (How many problems were completed correctly? What types of problems can the student answer?), teachers can better understand student thinking in order to differentiate instruction. Virtual manipulatives can also be used as a response to formative assessment as teachers make instructional decisions about which manipulatives to use and how to scaffold students' learning with virtual manipulatives. For example, the teacher could give a paper-based assessment of student learning or use results from a school-wide assessment to select appropriate manipulatives for individual instruction after gaps in student knowledge have been identified.

Summative Assessment

The other type of assessment common in classrooms is summative assessment. It relates to virtual manipulatives in two forms: online assessment and paper-based assessment. The first type may utilize the virtual environment itself to assess what students know. The second type utilizes other types of traditional paper-based assessments to see if students can transfer their learning in the virtual manipulative environment to other settings. A summative assessment can also be used to determine if students have integrated learning from the use of multiple types of virtual manipulatives.

For instance, if a teacher has used a set of manipulatives for arithmetic (e.g., Base-10 blocks, chips), the summative assessment can be used to determine what students have learned from the collective experience.

Designing Instruction Using Assessment

Moyer (this volume) describes two types of virtual manipulatives: open-ended explorations and guided-concept tutorials. Each type plays a different role in the assessment. For open-ended explorations, assessment should be used at the end of the activity to determine what students have learned and what they need to do next. Formative assessment can be used to guide the teacher's selection of open-ended explorations for groups or individual students. In a guided-concept tutorial, the virtual manipulative itself can become a formative assessment. Students' progress can be tracked and used as documentation of learning. Formative assessment can guide the selection of tutorials for students.

The fundamental questions in developing an assessment for a virtual manipulative are:

1. What concepts should students learn?
2. What concepts are important foundations for using the virtual manipulative?
3. How will the teacher know what the students have learned by using the virtual manipulative?
4. Does the virtual manipulative assess growth and development of knowledge? If so, how?

For the first question (what should students learn?), the teacher's goals for the lesson should be clear. Namely, the mathematical objectives should be clear. This helps the teacher both to select a virtual manipulative to use for an assessment and to assess students' learning from the virtual manipulative.

The second question asks about foundational knowledge. Is there knowledge that is prerequisite to using the virtual manipulative? Would it be helpful for students to have used a concrete manipulative before switching to the virtual manipulative in order to understand how the virtual manipulative operates? For assessment, the teacher does not want students' knowledge of mathematics to be confounded with their knowledge about what the virtual manipulative represents. For instance, do the students understand the difference between the types of blocks used in a Base-10 manipulative?

For the third question (how will the teacher know what students have learned?), the teacher needs to plan for and implement procedures for documenting what students have accomplished when using the virtual manipulative. In some cases, online documentation is available through the NLVM. The module will collect the data electronically as students submit responses and then the teacher can view a class's information. However, when electronic means are not available, the teacher will need another way to document what students have learned. This could also include situations where the students have used a series of virtual manipulatives and the teacher wants to know how the cumulative experience has impacted students' knowledge of the topic. In this case, students may complete paper-based quizzes or tests (Bolyard 2006; Suh 2005) to document what they learned. A similar assessment may be used at the beginning of the module in order to develop a baseline for students' understanding.

Self-Assessment and Student Feedback

The teacher has a significant role to play in terms of assessing student knowledge and learning. That role does not disappear when using virtual manipulatives. An advantage of virtual manipulatives, however, is that students can get immediate, instantaneous feedback about their answers. With paper-based activities and concrete manipulatives, students typically have to wait for the teacher to confirm their answer. In some of the virtual manipulative applets (e.g., adding fractions), students cannot proceed to the next level until they have answered the current problem correctly and they receive feedback about their progress. For example, in the Adding Fractions manipulative, the student receives feedback about each step immediately. Students can then proceed independently through the activities and work at their own pace. There is no requirement that all students in a class be at the same place (e.g., working on the same worksheet) when they are using virtual manipulatives.

Self-assessment is an important metacognitive and higher-order thinking ability (Lesh, Lester, and Hjalmarson 2003) that allows students to learn to assess their work on complex problem-solving tasks. Self-assessment scaffolds, embedded in many virtual manipulatives, allow a student to work independently by providing immediate step-by-step feedback (the Circle 0 game in Figure 3 shows when a circle includes the right sum as the values are moved onto the diagram). A number of the virtual manipulatives (particularly in geometry) are conducive to self-assessment by students. As

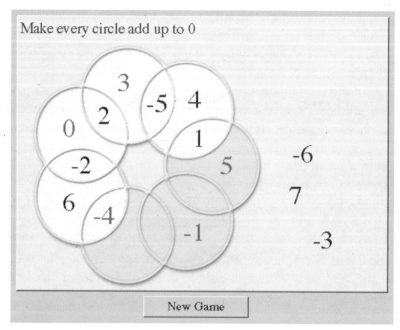

FIGURE 3 *NLVM applet Circle 0*
© 1999–2008 Utah State University

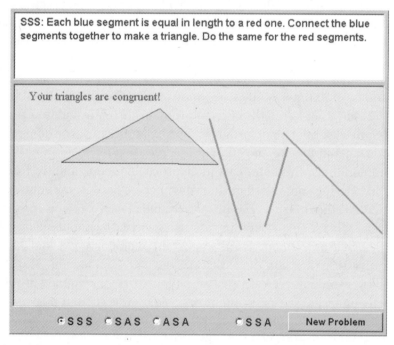

FIGURE 4 *NLVM applet Congruent Triangles*
© 1999–2008 Utah State University

the user moves pieces around the space, there are visual cues as to whether the answer is correct. For example, Figure 4 shows the Congruent Triangles manipulative. The students are given two sets of segments (red and blue) and have to create congruent triangles. When the segments are placed in a triangle, the triangle is filled in with a color. Students can then determine for themselves whether their answer is right or not before moving on to the next step.

Summary

Virtual manipulatives provide an opportunity for teachers to differentiate instruction easily using formative and summative assessments. In addition, virtual manipulatives can be used as assessments of students' learning, as teachers can track students' progress through problems. For students, many of the virtual manipulatives also provide ongoing and immediate feedback about their progress. Students can know whether they are right or wrong immediately as well as receiving feedback as they progress through an activity. In this way, virtual manipulatives are a tool for students' self-assessment as well as an assessment tool for teachers.

References

Black, P., C. Harrison, C. Lee, B. Marshall, and D. Wiliam. 2003. *Assessment for learning: Putting it into practice.* Berkshire, England: Open University Press.

Bolyard, J. J. 2006. A comparison of the impact of two virtual manipulatives on student achievement and conceptual understanding of integer addition and subtraction. *Dissertation Abstracts International* 66(11): 3960A.

Bush, W. S., and A. S. Greer. 1999. *Mathematics assessment: A practical handbook for grades 9–12.* Reston, VA: NCTM.

Lesh, R., F. K. Lester, and M. Hjalmarson. 2003. A models and modeling perspective on metacognitive functioning in everyday situations where mathematical constructs need to be developed. In R. A. Lesh and H. M. Doerr (Eds.), *Beyond constructivism: Models and modeling perspectives on mathematics problem solving, learning & teaching* (pp. 383–404). Hillsdale, NJ: Lawrence Erlbaum Associates.

Suh, J. M. 2005. *Third graders' mathematics achievement and representation preference using virtual and physical manipulatives for adding fractions and balancing equations.* Unpublished doctoral dissertation, George Mason University, Fairfax, VA.

Wiliam, D. 2008. Keeping learning on track: classroom assessment and the regulation of learning. In F. K. Lester (Ed.), *Second handbook of research on mathematics teaching and learning* (pp. 1051–1098). Charlotte, NC: Information Age Publishing.

Chapter 5

Virtual Manipulatives in Classroom Research

In this chapter, we discuss several examples of teachers participating in classroom action research using virtual manipulatives. Each example provides background information on the teaching of the lessons using virtual manipulatives, the methods that were used for data collection, brief findings from the classroom research, and how the classroom study informed instruction. The three classroom examples that follow feature classrooms in kindergarten, grade 3, and grade 6.

Studying Virtual Manipulatives in Kindergarten: A Classroom Example

Our first example comes from a classroom study on the topic of patterning that was conducted with a group of 18 kindergarten children in a Title I school, where over half of the students were Limited English Proficiency learners (Moyer, Niezgoda, and Stanley 2005). The children in the kindergarten were very experienced with creating a variety of types of patterns, and the teacher was interested in examining how the representational form (virtual manipulative pattern blocks, wooden pattern blocks, and student drawings) would influence the children's patterning behaviors.

The teacher planned three lessons on patterning for the children over a three-day span. During the first day, children created patterns using the wooden pattern blocks; the second day, they created patterns using the virtual manipulative pattern blocks; on the

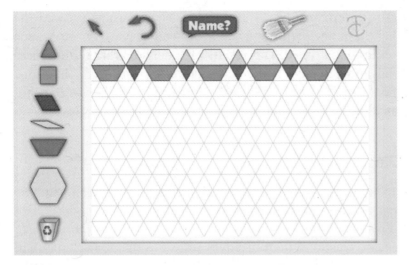

FIGURE I *Creative behaviors using the Arcytech applet Pattern Blocks*
© http://www.arcytech.org/java/patterns/patterns

third day, the children created patterns using drawing paper and multicolor markers. During the lessons, five observers recorded information about the patterns the children created by taking notes, drawing examples of the students' work, and printing copies of the children's work from the computer screen. After the three lessons, the teacher and the observers analyzed the children's work by looking at the types of patterns the children created, the number of patterns created, the number of blocks used in the whole pattern and in the pattern stems, and children's creative behaviors. For example, Figure 1 shows a repeating pattern in which the child created a blue triangle by using the green triangle to cover the blue rhombus, which was classified by the research team as a creative behavior.

How Did This Classroom Study Inform Instruction?

By looking at the patterns that the children created using each form of representation, the teacher was able to identify how the use of different representations influenced the patterns the children made. For example, the results showed that the children created a greater number of patterns, they used a greater number of blocks overall and in each pattern stem, and they exhibited more creative behaviors when they used the virtual manipulative pattern blocks (compared to the wooden pattern blocks or to the drawings). However, across each of the different forms of representation, children seemed to lose interest in the particular pattern they were creating once they reached a certain number of blocks or repeats of the pattern (approximately 13–16 blocks). These results showed the teacher that some patterning behaviors were consistent across each representational form. The results also demonstrated differences and advantages among the representations and that, therefore, teachers should choose different representational forms depending on their learning goals for a particular mathematics lesson.

A Classroom Example from Grade 3

In the next classroom study, the research was conducted with two groups of third-grade students learning concepts of addition of fractions and balancing equations (Suh 2005). For the third-grade lessons on fractions, the objectives were to rename fractions, find equivalent fractions, and add and subtract fractions with unlike denominators. Students used the Fraction Equivalent applet found on the National Library of Virtual Manipulatives (http://nlvm.usu. edu/en/nav/vlibrary.html) to explore relationships between equivalent fractions.

On the Fraction Equivalent applet, students were presented with fraction circles and squares with parts shaded, accompanied by the symbolic representation of the fraction, with the following directions: "Find a new name for this fraction by using the arrow buttons to set the number of pieces. Enter the new name and check your answer." Students clicked on arrow buttons below the whole unit, which changed the number of parts, to solve these problems. When students found an equivalent fraction, all lines turned red. When a common denominator was identified, students typed the names of the equivalent fractions into the appropriate boxes. They checked their answers by clicking the Check button. To help students explore relationships among equivalent fractions, the applet prompted students to find several equivalent fractions. This applet was specifically designed to develop the concept of renaming fractions.

Following the lesson on equivalent fractions, the third graders worked with the applet called Adding Fractions, also on the National Library of Virtual Manipulatives. This applet presented fractions with unlike denominators. The applet first prompted students to rename the fractions using the arrow button so that both fractions would have common denominators. Once students successfully renamed the fractions, students proceeded to the next screen to combine the fractions. (See Figure 2.) Students demonstrated significant gains in their knowledge of the algorithmic process for adding fractions with unlike denominators following their use of these virtual manipulative fraction applets.

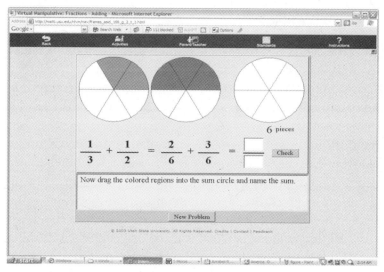

FIGURE 2   *NLVM applet Fractions – Adding*
© 1999–2008 Utah State University

During the second phase of this classroom study, students in the third grade were introduced to the concept of balancing linear equations using a dynamic algebra balance. During five one-hour class sessions, students used the dynamic algebra scale, which features balanced boxes that represent the unknown *x* and blocks that represent numbers. (See Figure 3.)

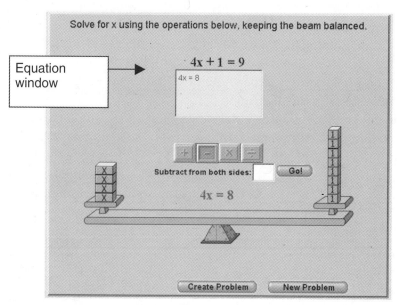

FIGURE 3   *NLVM applet Algebra Balance Scales*
© 1999–2008 Utah State University

1. After setting up the problem, students clicked on the minus sign and subtracted 1 block from both sides.
2. Once the 1 box disappeared from the screen, students chose the division sign and divided by 4 from each side.
3. Each step taken by the students (algorithm) was displayed in the equation window.

The third-grade students in this study had never been exposed to the concept of linear equations or to the use of a virtual balance scale. The pre- and posttest measures showed significant gains in students' knowledge of the algorithmic process for solving equations. One of the features of the virtual balance scale was that it explicitly linked the dynamic balance scale to the symbolic representation of the algebraic equations that were presented on the scale. When students typed in a symbolic command such as "subtract $3x$ from both sides," the dynamic feature of the applet removed three of the x boxes from both sides of the balance scale and simultaneously displayed a new equation on the screen. The equation window tracked moves made by the student, thereby scaffolding the process of solving for x and explicitly providing the connection between the equations and the actions of the balance scale. During the lessons, three observers collected data using videotaping, mini-interviews while students were working, and copies of students' work on recording sheets.

How Did This Classroom Study Inform Instruction?

There was much to be learned about teaching mathematics using the virtual manipulatives based on the experiences of these third-graders. When students used the Fraction Equivalent and Adding Fraction applets, the teacher noted that they had an opportunity to make sense of the algorithmic processes of combining fractions with unlike denominators. Research shows that students often encounter error patterns of "adding across" when adding fractions with unlike denominators, such as $\frac{1}{3} + \frac{1}{5} = \frac{2}{8}$ where they add the numerators, $1 + 1$, and the denominators, $3 + 5$ (Ashlock 2006). However, students who worked with the virtual fraction applets successfully renamed the fractions, as was modeled by the virtual fraction applet (e.g., $\frac{3}{4} + \frac{1}{8} = \frac{6}{8} + \frac{1}{8} = \frac{7}{8}$).

When using the virtual algebra balance scale, the teacher noticed that students were keenly aware of the simultaneous actions on the virtual scale and in the equation window. The link between students' actions and the corresponding actions of the onscreen objects and equations made the processes explicit for students.

In addition, the teacher noted that the dynamic capability of the tilting balance scale reinforced the concept of the equal sign, representing the equal sign to mean "the same as," rather than the common misconception of the equal sign meaning "the answer is" or "doing something." In this third-grade study, students' learning was enhanced significantly because they understood the concepts behind the procedures they were performing.

A Classroom Example from Grade 6

In our final example of a classroom study, the research was conducted with a group of 99 sixth-grade students studying operations with integers (Bolyard 2006). Four teachers and six classes of students from two middle schools participated in the study. The purpose of the investigation was to examine student learning outcomes following an instructional unit that used virtual manipulatives as a visual representation of integer addition and subtraction.

The instructional unit took place in four 90-minute sessions. Students explored concepts of integer addition and subtraction through either the context of money (debts and assets) or walking left and right along the number line. Introductory activities focused on establishing the concept of integers in these contexts using number lines and chips. After these introductory activities, students participated in extended computer lab sessions (30 to 40 minutes) in which they used virtual manipulatives representing either the number line or chips to explore addition and subtraction. (See Figures 4 and 5.)

Following each computer session, the teacher led students in follow-up discussions about what they had observed while working with the virtual manipulatives and any conjectures they had made. Students were encouraged to reaffirm and justify their conclusions. To determine changes in knowledge, students completed a pre- and posttest on integer addition and subtraction. In addition, at the end of the unit, a university researcher conducted task-based interviews with nine students. In these interviews, students represented and solved integer addition and subtraction scenarios using pictures, words, and numeric symbols.

How Did This Classroom Study Inform Instruction?
It was evident from the pre- and posttest scores of the students that students' skills in adding and subtracting integers had increased, particularly in the area of subtraction. In this area, pretest scores

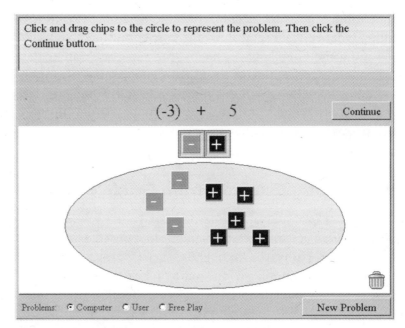

FIGURE 4 *NLVM applet Color Chips – Addition*
© 1999–2008 Utah State University

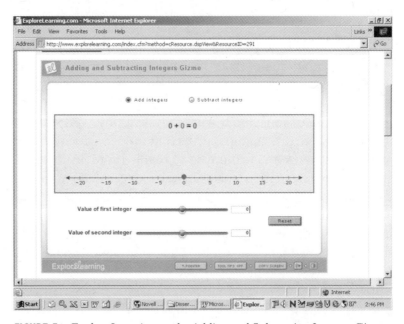

FIGURE 5 *ExploreLearning applet Adding and Subtracting Integers Gizmo*
© http://www.explorelearning.com

showed that students had little prior knowledge; posttest scores indicated that they had made significant gains at the end of the unit. Students' work and responses in the task-based interviews indicated that they were generally able to work with integers using various representational forms (symbols, words, and pictures), particularly for addition. For example, when given an integer addition problem in the form of a story, students could both write a number sentence and draw a picture to represent it. Students also used the different representational forms to help them reason through a given task, explain their thinking, and detect and correct errors in their work.

However, there was evidence that students had more difficulty translating between actions describing or representing subtraction (either in a story or in a picture) and the symbolic form of the problem. For example, when working with a story scenario that described a situation such as $(-9) - (-3)$, students interpreted this either as subtraction $(-9 - -3)$ or as an equivalent addition scenario $(-9 + 3)$ and used these interpretations to evaluate the story and draw a corresponding picture. However, when it came time to write the number sentence, several students who had interpreted the problem as $-9 + 3$ wrote the number sentence $-9 - 3$. They understood the action of the story (that subtracting a negative number is equivalent to adding its opposite), but they were unable to translate this to symbols, focusing only on the value of the integers and not on how the operation sign determined that value. This indicates that, while students made gains in their understanding of integer addition and subtraction after using the virtual models, additional work needed to be done to solidify the connection between stories and pictures representing subtraction situations and the role of the subtraction sign in the number sentence that corresponds to those scenarios.

Summary

As these classroom research projects show, teachers can gain a great deal of information from examining their own practices while using virtual manipulatives in a mathematics classroom. These teaching experiments can be useful, not only for the teachers conducting the action research themselves, but also for other educators who are making choices about how to integrate virtual manipulatives and other technology tools into their classrooms.

References

Ashlock, R. B. 2006. *Error patterns in computation: Using error patterns to improve instruction*, 9th edition. Upper Saddle River, NJ: Merrill Prentice Hall.

Bolyard, J. J. 2006. A comparison of the impact of two virtual manipulatives on student achievement and conceptual understanding of integer addition and subtraction. *Dissertation Abstracts International* 66(11): 3960A.

Moyer, P. S., D. Niezgoda, and J. Stanley. 2005. Young children's use of virtual manipulatives and other forms of mathematical representations. In W. J. Masalski and P. C. Elliott (Eds.), *Technology-supported mathematics learning environments: Sixty-seventh yearbook* (pp. 17–34). Reston, VA: NCTM.

Suh, J. M. 2005. *Third graders' mathematics achievement and representation preference using virtual and physical manipulatives for adding fractions and balancing equations*. Doctoral dissertation, George Mason University, Fairfax, VA.

Chapter 6

Technical Information for Using the Virtual Manipulatives Library

*T*his chapter provides technical information about using the NLVM virtual manipulatives (http://nlvm.usu.edu/en/nav/vlibrary.html). Before using any of the virtual manipulatives with students, teachers should become familiar with their technical features. Some features are common to all virtual manipulatives; other features are specific to certain virtual manipulatives. Teachers should also know how to save and print student work to keep as a permanent record of students' explorations with the virtual manipulatives. Finally, this chapter summarizes the tools found on eNLVM, a complement to the National Library of Virtual Manipulatives.

Overview of the National Library of Virtual Manipulatives Home Page

When you first arrive at the National Library of Virtual Manipulatives home page, you'll notice a two-dimensional grid, which is divided into mathematical strands on the vertical axis (Number & Operations, Algebra, Geometry, Measurement, and Data Analysis & Probability), and grade-level bands on the horizontal axis (PreK–2, 3–5, 6–8, 9–12). (See Figure 1.) To search for a particular virtual manipulative by strand and grade level, simply navigate your cursor to the intersection of those two fields. For example, to search for algebra virtual manipulatives at the 3–5 grade level, place the cursor in the appropriate intersecting cell. You may also click on the Search button to see the list of all applets in the virtual library.

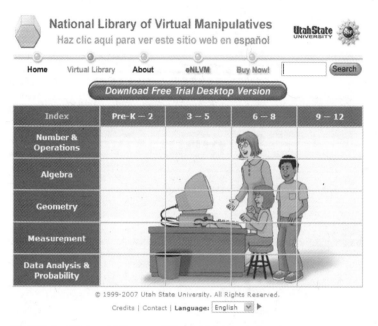

FIGURE 1 *National Library of Virtual Manipulatives home page*
© 1999–2008 Utah State University

Certain manipulatives can be found in multiple grade-level bands, as well as in multiple strands. For example, the Base Blocks virtual manipulative can be found in Algebra 3–5, Algebra 6–8, and Algebra 9–12, as well as in Number & Operations PreK–2, 3–5, and 6–8.

Once you have selected a virtual manipulative, the manipulative will open in the same window (or in some cases, a new window). To return to the main search page, select Back from the toolbar located above the virtual manipulative.

You can also search for a particular strand across all grade levels. To do so, click on the specific strand, such as Number & Operations, on the vertical axis. The resulting display will include all Number & Operations virtual manipulatives, grouped by grade level. Similarly, to search for all strands within a particular grade level, click on the specific grade band, such as 3–5, on the horizontal axis. The resulting display will include all grade 3–5 virtual manipulatives, grouped by grade band.

Features of Each Virtual Manipulative

Once you have selected a particular virtual manipulative and it has opened (either in the same or a new window), you'll see four buttons on the upper toolbar of the new screen: Back, Parent/Teacher, Standards, and Instructions.

- The Back button returns you to the previous screen.
- When you click the Parent/Teacher button, you will see specific information (including technical advice) for using the virtual manipulatives on the right side of the window, as well as helpful hints and suggestions for questions to ask students.
- The Standards button takes you to the National Council of Teachers of Mathematics (NCTM) Content Standards for that grade level and strand.
- Finally, the Instructions button provides specific activities that can be completed by students using that particular virtual manipulative.

The off-line version of the NLVM includes three additional buttons on the toolbar: Print, Open, and Save. Many of the virtual manipulatives also include an Activities button, which allows users to scroll through several options of exploratory activities for each individual applet.

Special Features of Select Virtual Manipulatives

In addition to the common features previously discussed, some virtual manipulatives offer specific features for enhancing their use. For example, the Fractions – Adding applet (in Number & Operations) lets you set one of three difficulty levels—Easier, Harder, Hardest—by clicking on the radio buttons at the bottom of the screen. (See Figure 2.) In this case, you can address a wide range of ability levels within the classroom by altering the difficulty levels.

Another feature afforded by some of the virtual manipulatives is the ability to select computer-generated values, or for the user to enter his or her own values. For example, the Factor Tree virtual manipulative (in Number & Operations) allows the user to factor computer-generated numbers or any number he or she selects. (See Figure 3.) In addition, for this particular applet, the user may choose to complete one factor tree or two factor trees simultaneously.

Some virtual manipulatives let students move or slide components of the tools. For example, several geometry applets let students rotate an object or look at the object from multiple views. A student using the Platonic Solids – Slicing tool, in the Geometry strand, can click and drag on the slider to change the view of intersection. (See Figure 4.)

Other geometry virtual manipulatives offer similar features. The slider on both the Platonic Solids and Platonic Solids – Dual (in Geometry) lets students resize the three-dimensional objects. By pointing the mouse at one of the vertices of the solid and mov-

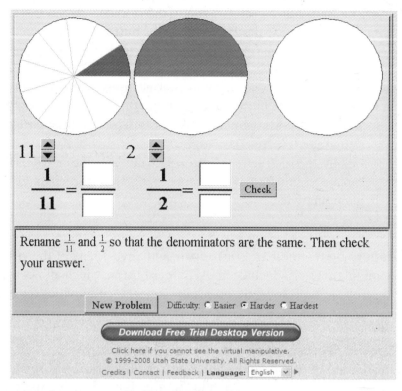

FIGURE 2 *NLVM applet Fractions – Adding*
© 1999–2008 Utah State University

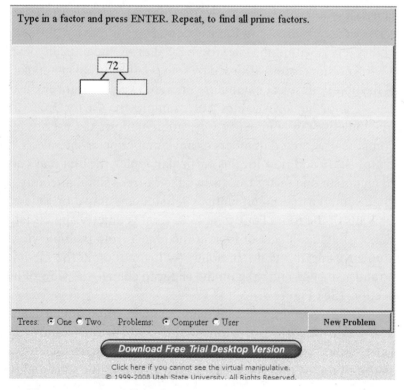

FIGURE 3 *NLVM applet Factor Tree*
© 1999–2008 Utah State University

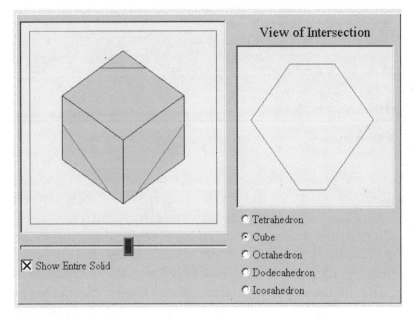

FIGURE 4 *NLVM applet Platonic Solids – Slicing*
© 1999–2008 Utah State University

ing the mouse around the screen, students can also rotate the object. Before using any of the virtual manipulatives with students, explore the specific technical features of each manipulative yourself to decide how you can best use the applet during instruction.

How to Print from the Website Using Screen Shots

As a means of recording their work, students may wish to create screen shots of their explorations with the virtual manipulatives. Simply put, a screen shot is a camera image of what is on the computer screen at a given moment in time. Multiple, successive screen shots can capture various steps taken by students as they work. The

---

1. Hold down the **APPLE, SHIFT**, and **4** keys.
2. When the target symbol appears, use the mouse to draw a frame around your graph.
3. Your graph will be saved to the desktop as "Picture 1."
4. Open this file and print.
5. Rename and save to desired directory.

FIGURE 5 *Instructions for saving and printing student work on a Mac*

1. Press the **PRINT SCREEN** key.
2. Your graph will be saved in the clipboard.
3. Open the computer's Paint program.
4. Paste picture into Paint.
5. Print.
6. Save as a Paint document.

FIGURE 6 *Instructions for saving and printing student work on a PC*

steps for saving and printing work are shown in Figure 5 (for Mac) and Figure 6 (for PCs). Before they create screen shots of their work, have students practice on any virtual manipulative.

Note that students working on a PC, rather than pasting the picture into Paint, may paste screen shots into a word processing document, particularly if they want to record notes in typewritten form. To print the screen when using the off-line version of the virtual manipulatives library, simply click on the Print button; to save the image, simply click on the Save button, type in a name, and click on Save an Image File.

Using the Virtual Manipulatives with SMART Boards

When you use virtual manipulatives with the entire class, a SMART Board may be beneficial. One feature you may want to capitalize on is the dual-page feature, which projects a virtual manipulative on one side of the screen (while still permitting interaction with the virtual manipulative), and a white board on the other side of the screen. Because the virtual manipulative and white board appear simultaneously, you and your students can write notes next to the virtual manipulatives images.

Features Available through eNLVM

By registering for the enhanced National Library of Virtual Manipulatives (eNLVM), which you can find at http://enlvm.usu.edu/ma/nav/doc/intro.jsp, you can benefit from a project funded by the National Science Foundation that enriches the eNLVM. (See Figure 7.) eNLVM offers four unique features: eModules, Tracking Tools, Adaptation Tools, and Collaboration Tools.

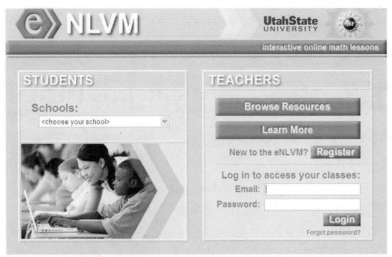

FIGURE 7 *eNLVM registration page*
© 1999–2008 Utah State University

- *eModules* are learning units designed for Grades 2 through 7 in pre-algebra, algebra I and II, geometry, precalculus, and trigonometry. Each of these units incorporates virtual manipulatives in lesson plans and offers assessment options.
- *Tracking Tools* allow students to submit their answers while they are working with the virtual manipulatives. Teachers can then view summaries of their students' responses, as well as students' individual responses.
- *Adaptation Tools* give teachers the opportunity to adapt and modify lessons and activities to meet the needs of their students. Using this feature, teachers can reorganize and modify activities, as well as instructions, questions, and the configurations of the virtual manipulatives.
- *Collaboration Tools* let teachers share materials with other teachers, who can then adopt and modify these resources to meet the needs of their own students.

Whole Number Addition Using Base-10 Blocks

Grade-Level Band

Pre K–2

Discussion of the Mathematics

In this lesson, students use virtual Base-10 blocks to solve addition problems with two-digit numbers. The students join ten unit blocks together to form one ten-block (long) while solving addition problems. This concept is then applied to paper-and-pencil addition problems.

NCTM Standards

Number & Operations

- Use multiple models to develop initial understandings of place value and the Base-10 number system
- Develop a sense of whole numbers and represent and use them in flexible ways, including relating, composing, and decomposing numbers
- Connect numerals to the quantities they represent, using various physical models and representations
- Understand the effects of adding whole numbers
- Develop and use strategies for whole-number computations, with a focus on addition

- Use a variety of methods and tools to compute, including objects, mental computation, estimation, paper and pencil, and calculators

Lesson Objectives

Upon successful completion of this lesson, the student will be able to:

- Represent a two-digit number using virtual Base-10 blocks
- Solve addition problems using virtual Base-10 blocks
- Join ten ones together to form one ten

Virtual Manipulatives Websites

National Library of Virtual Manipulatives for Interactive Mathematics: http://nlvm.usu.edu/en/nav/vlibrary.html

Grade Band PreK–2, Number & Operations, Base Blocks: http://nlvm.usu.edu/en/nav/frames_asid_152_g_1_t_1.html

Grade Band PreK–2, Number & Operations, Base Blocks Addition: http://nlvm.usu.edu/en/nav/frames_asid_154_g_1_t_1.html

Materials

- A computer with an LCD projector for demonstration
- A computer with Internet connection for each student
- "Whole Number Addition" activity sheet for each student

Mathematical Vocabulary

addition, ones, tens, place value, regroup

Activity and Teacher Notes

Approximate Duration of the Lesson
60 minutes

Warm-Up Discussion
Using an LCD projector and computer with Internet access, go to the *National Library of Virtual Manipulatives*. Click on the inter-

section of *Grade Band Pre-K–2* and *Number & Operations*. Then click on "Base Blocks." Use the arrows to change the number of columns to 2 (lower right-hand side).

Ask the students how you could show the number 32. How many tens are in 32? (Click on the blue icon at the top of the Tens column to enter three ten-longs.) How many ones are in 32? (Click on the blue icon at the top of the Ones column to enter two ones.) Count the blocks with the students (10, 20, 30, 31, 32). Click on the *Clear* button (top right) to clear the screen. Do the same activity for the numbers 15 and 28. Clear the screen.

Click on the icon above the Ones column to enter 13 ones. Ask the students how many groups of ten can be made using these blocks. How many leftover ones will there be? Show the students how to lasso ten of the blocks. To lasso the blocks, students should left click in the area of the blocks, which will create a rectangle that can be used to surround ten blocks. After the 10 ones blocks move together to create one ten-long, move the ten-long into the Tens column. Use the process of *counting on* (i.e., 10, 11, 12, 13) to count the blocks with the students. Clear the screen. Do the same activity for the numbers 16 and 23.

Model the Activity

Click the Back button (top left) to return to the list of *Grade Band Pre-K–2 Number & Operations* virtual manipulatives. Click on Base Blocks Addition. Use the arrows to change the number of columns to 2 (lower right-hand side). Click on Next Problem. Ask students to estimate the sum. Will it be more than 30? 50? Why do you think so? Model how to solve the problem by using the lasso feature to make a ten-long. Move the ten-long over to the Tens column. Model two or three problems.

Click on Create Problem. Model how to create the problem 27 + 25. (Click on the icons at the top of the Tens and Ones columns to enter 2 tens and 5 ones. Move the blocks down into the lower space. Then enter 2 tens and 7 ones. The computer will show 27 + 25.)

Click Begin Problem. Ask the students if you can lasso a ten. How many ones will be left over? Move ten ones together and lasso them to create a ten-long. Move the long into the Tens column. Model the procedure for the problem 35 + 29.

Tell students that they will first solve addition problems that the computer generates and then create their own problems on the computer. Give each student an activity sheet and briefly discuss the three parts. Tell students that they can use the virtual Base-10 blocks to help them solve the addition problems on the activity sheet. There is also space where they can record problems that they have created on their own.

Students Work Individually
Allow 10 minutes for students to solve computer-created problems. Circulate as students work to check for understanding.

Teacher Tip
If the problems the computer presents get too difficult, back arrow out and return to base blocks addition. This will reset the program to easier problems. Some students may have difficulty drawing a box around ten blocks. They may need to make their boxes bigger. It is also helpful to move the blocks closer together before attempting to lasso them.

After 10 minutes, direct students to begin solving the problems on the activity sheet. Remind them to click on the Create Problem button. Circulate as students work. Check for student understanding. Are students using the virtual Base-10 blocks to solve the addition problems? Are they solving the problems without using the virtual Base-10 blocks? As students complete the problems on the activity sheet, direct them to create their own problems on the computer and record them on the activity sheet.

Follow-Up Discussion
Gather students in a central meeting area. Have the LCD projector and computer available for use. Ask students to explain the process of adding two-digit numbers.

- What do you do first? Second?
- Do you always need to regroup?
- When do you regroup?
- When don't you regroup?

Have a few students share problems they created on their own. Ask the other students to estimate the answers. Then have the student who created the problem model how to solve the problem either with or without virtual Base-10 blocks.

Student Assessment

- Can the student use virtual Base-10 blocks to represent a given number? Does the student use tens and ones or all ones?

- Can the student tell how many groups of ten are in a two-digit number? (e.g., 13 has one group of ten and three extra ones)
- Can the student explain the process of adding two-digit numbers?
- Can the student add two-digit numbers without using the virtual Base-10 blocks?

What to Expect from Students

A portion of student work on the Activity Sheet is shown in Figure 1.

How many blocks?

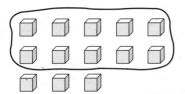 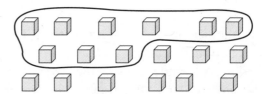

How many groups of ten? __1__   How many groups of ten? __1__

How many leftover ones? __3__   How many leftover ones? __9__

FIGURE 1 *A portion of student work on the activity sheet*

Extensions and Connections

Have students add three- or four-digit numbers by changing the number of columns on the virtual Base-10 blocks.

Whole Number Addition

How many blocks?

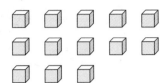

How many groups of ten? ___   How many groups of ten? ___

How many leftover ones? ___   How many leftover ones? ___

Find the sums.

27	45	38	19	26
+ 25	+ 35	+ 47	+ 12	+ 48

Create your own addition problems.

+ _____   + _____   + _____   + _____

Fraction Pictures of Multiplication

Grade-Level Band

3–5

Discussion of the Mathematics

This lesson is an introduction to multiplication of fractions. Area models are used to demonstrate conceptually what it means to multiply fractions. Students will use a virtual area model to demonstrate, explore, and practice multiplication of fractions.

NCTM Standards

Number & Operations

- Develop understanding of fractions as parts of unit wholes
- Understand various meanings of multiplication
- Develop and use strategies to estimate computations involving fractions in situations relevant to students' experience

Lesson Objectives

On successfully completing this lesson, the student will be able to:

- Use an area model to multiply fractions

Virtual Manipulatives Websites

National Library of Virtual Manipulatives for Interactive Mathematics: http://nlvm.usu.edu/en/nav/vlibrary.html
Grade Band 3–5, Number & Operations, Fractions – Rectangular Multiplication:
http://nlvm.usu.edu/en/nav/frames_asid_194_g_2_t_1.html

Materials

- Computer with Internet connection for every two students
- LCD projector hooked up to a computer or SMART Board
- "Fraction Pictures of Multiplication" activity sheet for each student
- Chalkboard and chalk (white and colored chalk)
- White lined paper
- Colored pencils and/or crayons

Mathematical Vocabulary

fraction, multiply, numerator, denominator

Activity and Teacher Notes

Approximate Duration of the Lesson
One hour and 15 minutes (or two 45-minute lessons)

Warm-Up Discussion
Give each student a piece of paper.

On the board, write a whole-number multiplication expression (e.g., 2×3, 6×8). Ask students how they can visually represent the expression and have them draw their representations on the paper. Ask several students to draw their representations on the board.

After several representations have been given and it is clear that students understand how the array model can be used to represent multiplication, write the expression $2 \times \frac{1}{3}$ on the board. Again have the students draw their representations on paper and share them. For example, here is a student's representation for $2 \times \frac{1}{3}$.

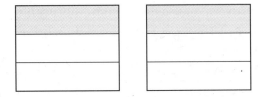

Finally, write the expressions $\frac{1}{2} \times \frac{1}{3}$ and $\frac{1}{4} \times \frac{2}{5}$ on the board. Explain to the students that today they will learn how to visually represent these expressions. First, they will use a computer graphic and then they will transfer it to paper.

Teacher Tip

You may want to set the multiplication in a context. A garden works well for the area model. If half the garden is planted with roses and one-third of the garden is planted with red flowers, how much of the garden is planted with red roses? It may also be useful to have the students verbalize the multiplication as ___ of ___. For example, $\frac{1}{2} \times \frac{1}{4}$ is one-half of one-fourth.

Model the Activity

Using the computer and projector screen, go to the *National Library of Virtual Manipulatives* website (http://nlvm.usu.edu/nav/vlibrary.html), click on *Grade Band 3–5, Number & Operations*, and then click on "Fractions – Rectangular Multiplication."

With the settings on the bottom as Proper Fractions and Show Me, demonstrate how to use the virtual manipulative. Make sure the students understand how to change the denominator and then move the cursor to highlight the needed fraction.

Teacher Tip

If you set one of the fractions to $\frac{0}{1}$, you can show just one fraction in the fraction square. This may be helpful when students are just beginning to use the manipulative. Set the red fraction to $\frac{0}{1}$. Show the fraction represented by the blue section. Have the students count the sections (shown as the denominator) and the number of sections that are shaded (shown as the numerator). Then set the blue fraction to $\frac{0}{1}$. Discuss the fraction represented by the red section. Then show both fractions together. The overlap is the result of multiplying the two fractions.

Students Work with Partners

When it appears that the students understand, have them move to their own computers (two students to each computer).

Together, using the projector, guide the students to the site. Allow students to use the Show Me option to get warmed up. When they are ready, move on to the Test Me option. (Make sure students set the graphic to the given fraction equation but give their answer before clicking on the Check button.)

While the students are working, walk around and check for understanding.

Once the students have had plenty of time to work with the virtual manipulative, have them leave the computers and come back together as a class.

Follow-Up Discussion

Ask the students what they noticed when they multiplied two fractions. Some may observe that the product gets smaller and that all you do is multiply the numerators and then multiply the denominators.

Make sure the students understand both of those observations before moving on.

Students Work Independently

Hand out the "Fraction Pictures of Multiplication" activity sheet.

Explain that now the students are going to draw representations of the fractions multiplication equations.

Each student needs two different colored pencils or crayons (e.g., yellow and blue or red and blue).

Model the first problem on the board. Then have students do the second problem and go over it together before asking them to complete the rest of the activity sheet.

Student Assessment

- Can the student accurately represent the fractions using an area model?
- Can the student explain the area model?
- Can the student multiply fractions without using an area model?

What to Expect from Students

$$1. \frac{1}{4} \times \frac{1}{2} = \underline{\frac{1}{8}}$$

$$2. \frac{1}{2} \times \frac{1}{3} = \underline{\frac{1}{6}}$$

$$3. \frac{1}{2} \times \frac{1}{5} = \underline{\frac{1}{10}}$$

FIGURE I *Sample student work from the Fraction Pictures of Multiplication Activity Sheet, with responses*

Extensions and Connections

After students have mastered multiplying two proper fractions, they can move on to multiplying improper fractions (or fractions greater than one). To do that, students simply need to change the options on the virtual manipulative to Improper Fractions.

Fraction Pictures of Multiplication

Directions: Use the squares to make a diagram to find the product. Use two different colors to help you find the product.

1. $\dfrac{1}{4} \times \dfrac{1}{2} =$ _____

2. $\dfrac{1}{2} \times \dfrac{1}{3} =$ _____

3. $\dfrac{1}{2} \times \dfrac{1}{5} =$ _____

4. $\dfrac{2}{5} \times \dfrac{1}{2} =$ _____

5. $\dfrac{1}{4} \times \dfrac{1}{3} =$ _____

6. $\dfrac{3}{4} \times \dfrac{1}{2} =$ _____

7. $\dfrac{2}{3} \times \dfrac{2}{6} =$ _____

8. $\dfrac{2}{3} \times \dfrac{3}{7} =$ _____

9. $\dfrac{3}{4} \times \dfrac{2}{3} =$ _____

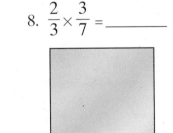

Now find the products without using a diagram.

11. $\dfrac{2}{5} \times \dfrac{1}{2} =$ _____

12. $\dfrac{3}{7} \times \dfrac{2}{3} =$ _____

13. $\dfrac{5}{6} \times \dfrac{1}{8} =$ _____

Fraction Pictures of Multiplication Activity

Sample Lesson 3:
Number & Operations

Adding Integers

Grade-Level Band

6–8

Discussion of the Mathematics

In this lesson, students will use virtual color chips to solve addition problems involving integers (i.e., the set of whole numbers and their opposites). Students will explore the effects of adding two positive numbers, two negative numbers, a negative number and a positive number, a positive number and zero, and a negative number and zero. Students will need to be introduced to positive and negative numbers and to understand the concept of *absolute value* before participating in this lesson.

NCTM Standards

Number & Operations

- Develop meaning for integers and represent and compare quantities with them
- Understand the meaning and effects of arithmetic operations with integers

Lesson Objectives

On successfully completing this lesson, the student will be able to:

- Add integers
- Identify the effects of adding two negative numbers, two positive numbers, a negative number and a positive number, and so on

Virtual Manipulatives Websites

National Library of Virtual Manipulatives for Interactive Mathematics: http://nlvm.usu.edu/en/nav/vlibrary.html
Grade Band 3–5, Number & Operations, Color Chips – Addition: http://nlvm.usu.edu/en/nav/frames_asid_161_g_2_t_1.html

Materials

- A computer with an LCD projector for demonstration
- One computer, with Internet connection, for each student
- "Adding Integers" activity sheet for each student

Mathematical Vocabulary

addition, integers, positive, negative, absolute value

Activity and Teacher Notes

Approximate Duration of the Lesson
60 minutes

Warm-Up Discussion
To begin the lesson, review positive and negative numbers by asking the following questions. Students may say that positive numbers are to the right of 0 on a number line and that negative numbers are to the left of 0 on a number line.

- What is an integer?
- What is a positive number? A negative number?

- Where are the positive numbers located on the number line? The negative numbers?

Next, review the concept of absolute value by having students respond to the following questions. Students should recall that absolute value is the distance from zero on a number line.

- What is the absolute value of –6? (6)
- What is the absolute value of +7? (7)
- What is the absolute value of 0? (0)
- Which has a greater absolute value: –8 or +3? (–8)

Distribute the "Adding Integers" activity sheet to each student. Have students complete Section A of the activity sheet before continuing.

Model the Activity

Using an LCD projector and computer, go to the *National Library of Virtual Manipulatives*. Click on *Grade Band 3–5, Number & Operations*, and then click on "Color Chips – Addition."

The screen will automatically provide a computer-generated addition problem involving two integers. Model for students how to use the virtual manipulative to add two integers:

1. Click and drag chips to the circle (oval) to represent the problem. Then click the Continue button.
2. Simplify by dragging minus (negative) chips onto plus (positive) chips.
3. Type in the answer and click the Check button.

Repeat this for several computer-generated problems.

Show the students how to change the activity by clicking on User at the bottom of the screen. Ask a student to make up an addition problem using integers. Type the two integers in the boxes provided and click Continue. Model how to solve the problem as before.

Tell students that they will first solve addition problems that the computer generates and then create their own problems. Briefly discuss the remaining three parts of the activity sheet (Sections B, C, and D). Tell students that they can use the virtual chips to help them record, solve, and create the addition problems on the activity sheet.

Individual Student Work on the Computers

Allow 10 minutes for students to solve computer-generated problems. Circulate as students work to check for understanding. Students should record at least four computer-generated problems in Section B of the activity sheet.

After 10 minutes, direct students to begin creating the problems described in Section C of activity sheet. Remind them to click on the *User* button. Circulate as students work. Check for student understanding. Are students using the virtual chips to solve the addition problems? Are they creating each of the six types of problems suggested in Section C? As students create their own problems on the computer, direct them to record the problems on the activity sheet. Students may wish to create drawings of the problem as they are first presented by the computer, or they may wish to record one of the steps involved in solving the integer problems. Students should choose the representation that is most useful to them.

You may also wish to have students create and record multiple equations for each of the scenarios in Section C. This would allow them to see a pattern.

Follow-Up Discussion

Gather students in a central meeting area. Have the LCD projector and computer available for use. Ask students to explain the process of adding integers.

Have a few students share problems they created on their own. Ask the other students to calculate the answers. Then have the student who created the problem model how to solve the problem either with or without virtual chips.

Students should complete Section D of the activity sheet, in which they compare their predictions (from Section A) to their work (from Section C). To initiate a discussion, you may wish to write a number of equations on the board, for a negative plus a negative (for example), and then ask, "Do you think the answer will always be negative?" This will help students think about what's happening. Repeat for each of the other types of problems.

Student Assessment

- Can the student use virtual chips to represent a given addition problem?
- Can the student add integers without using the virtual chips?
- Can the student explain the results of various types of addition problems involving integers?

What to Expect from Students

Sample student work, from Section C of the Adding Integers activity sheet, is shown in Figure 1.

3. a positive and a negative number, where the positive number has a greater absolute value

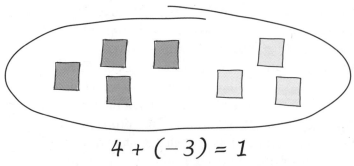

$$4 + (-3) = 1$$

4. a positive and a negative number, where the negative number has a greater absolute value

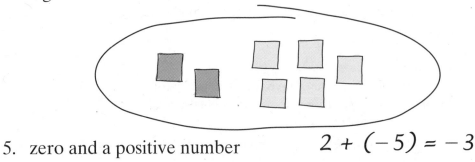

5. zero and a positive number $2 + (-5) = -3$

FIGURE I   *Sample student work, from Section C of the Adding Integers activity sheet*

Extensions and Connections

Have students use one of the following extension activities, as found in the National Library of Virtual Manipulatives:

> Grade Band 3–5, Number & Operations, Circle 0:
>
> http://nlvm.usu.edu/en/nav/frames_asid_122_g_3_t_1.html
>
> Grade Band 3–5, Number & Operations, Circle 21:
>
> http://nlvm.usu.edu/en/nav/frames_asid_188_g_3_t_1.html
>
> Grade Band 3–5, Number & Operations, Circle 99:
>
> http://nlvm.usu.edu/en/nav/frames_asid_269_g_3_t_1.html

In each puzzle, students place integers inside circles to sum to a certain number (0, 21, or 99).

Adding Integers

A. Prior to using the virtual manipulative, predict the *sign* of the sum of each of the following addition problems:

   1.   two positive numbers _____

   2.   two negative numbers _____

   3.   a positive and a negative number, where the positive number has a greater absolute value _____

   4.   a positive and a negative number, where the negative number has a greater absolute value _____

   5.   zero and a positive number _____

   6.   zero and a negative number _____

B. Use the virtual manipulative to act out and record at least four different computer-generated problems. Be sure to draw a picture of the red and black chips, as shown on your computer screen.

   1.

   2.

3.

4.

C. Use the virtual manipulative to act out and record the following types of problems. (You will need to click on "User" for the type of problems.) Be sure to draw a picture of the red and black chips, as shown on your computer screen.

1. two positive numbers

2. two negative numbers

3. a positive and a negative number, where the positive number has a greater absolute value

4. a positive and a negative number, where the negative number has a greater absolute value

5. zero and a positive number

6. zero and a negative number

D. Compare the results of Section C with your predictions in Section A. Were you correct? Did your thinking change as a result of this lesson? What did you learn in this lesson about adding integers?

Beads Everywhere!

Grade-Level Band

PreK–2

Discussion of the Mathematics

In this lesson, students recognize, compare, and analyze patterns. Class discussion focuses on the idea that a pattern is something that happens over and over again. Students describe patterns that are generated on the Color Patterns Website and translate them into simple motion patterns. Students then extend the patterns that are created by the virtual pattern generator. Finally, students create and describe their own patterns.

NCTM Standards

Algebra

- Recognize, describe, and extend patterns such as sequences of sounds and shapes or simple numeric patterns and translate from one representation to another;
- Analyze how repeating patterns are generated

Lesson Objectives

Upon successful completion of this lesson, the student will be able to:

- Recognize, describe, and extend patterns
- Create repeating patterns
- Identify stems of simple repeating patterns
- Translate color patterns to motion patterns
- Compare patterns

Virtual Manipulatives Websites

National Library of Virtual Manipulatives for Interactive Mathematics: http://nlvm.usu.edu/en/nav/vlibrary.html

Grade Band K–2, Algebra, Color Patterns:
http://nlvm.usu.edu/en/nav/frames_asid_184_g_1_t_2.html

Materials

- A computer with an LCD projector for demonstration
- A computer with Internet connection for every two students
- "Beads Everywhere" activity sheet for each student
- Crayons or colored pencils

Mathematical Vocabulary

pattern, repeat, stem

Activity and Teacher Notes

Approximate Duration of the Lesson
60 minutes

Warm-Up Discussion
Using a computer with an LCD projector, go to the *National Library of Virtual Manipulatives*. Click on the intersection of *Grade Band Pre-K–2* and *Algebra*. Click on "Color Patterns." Click on New Problem until a very easy pattern appears (one with only two colors). Ask students to tell a neighbor what color would come next. Then have one student share what the next color would be. Ask: How do you know that ____ comes next? (A typical answer would be "because blue always comes after yellow.") Continue in this way until the pattern is complete. Show the students how to click on "Check Answer" to see if the pattern was completed correctly.

Tell students that the "stem" of the pattern is the part that repeats over and over again. Ask students what the stem of this pattern is.

Have the class translate the pattern into a motion pattern. For example, if the pattern on the screen is "red, blue, red, blue, . . ." the class could clap for red and pat for blue. So the pattern is "clap, pat, clap, pat, . . ." Continue doing the motion pattern until every student in the class has caught on, and the whole class is doing the motions together.

Click on New Problem to generate another incomplete pattern. Repeat the activities for one or two more patterns. Then have students go to their own computers to continue the lesson.

Teacher Tip

If possible, each student should have access to his/her own computer.

Students Work Individually

Direct students to the Color Pattern Website. The Website will automatically create patterns for the students. Students should click on the color that best continues the pattern until all the question mark circles are filled in. They should then click Check Answer to see if they are correct. Students should continue by clicking on New Problem. Allow about 10 minutes for students to work on the Website.

Observe and ask questions to monitor student understanding of patterns as they work. Ask: How did you know which color came next? What is the stem of this pattern? How would you describe the pattern?

Students Work with Partners

Assign a partner to each student. Have partners work together in the following way. Each student creates a pattern on his or her "Beads Everywhere!" activity sheet by coloring in the circles, leaving the circles with question marks in them blank. Partners then swap papers and finish the pattern their partner created. When both patterns are complete, students can work together to write brief descriptions of the patterns. They might also include statements about how the two patterns are the same and different.

Follow-Up Discussion

Ask partners to share the patterns they created. Have students show the completed patterns and describe them in words. As each pair of students shares, ask some of the following questions: What is the stem of your pattern? How is your pattern the same as your partner's pattern? How is your pattern different from your partner's pattern? What was easy (hard) about finishing the pattern your partner made? How did you figure out the next color in the pattern? Do you think there might be more than one way to continue the pattern? Why or why not? In addition, have all students translate some of the shared patterns into motion patterns.

Student Assessment

- Can the student extend a repeating pattern?
- Can the student create a repeating pattern?
- Can the student translate a pattern into motions?
- Can the student describe a pattern in words?
- Can the student identify the stem of a pattern?
- Can the student compare two patterns?
- What is the level of sophistication of the pattern the student is able to extend/create? Can the student extend/create an A-B pattern? Can the student extend/create an A-B-C pattern? Can the student extend/create patterns with more than two colors or patterns with greater sophistication than A-B (such as A-A-B or A-B-C-B)?

What to Expect from Students

- Students should say the color names to help them hear the repeating sounds of the color names in the pattern.
- Students may figure out on their own how to erase mistakes. If not, you will need to help them do so. (Click on the bead with the mistake, and it will go back to a question mark.)

Extensions and Connections

- Note that this lesson is geared toward a first-grade class. Kindergarten teachers would benefit from using concrete models before teaching the lesson using the virtual manipulative.
- Pair students up. Give each pair of students a piece of string or yarn and a selection of colored beads. Have the pair work

together to create a pattern. On a piece of construction paper, they can draw a representation of their pattern. Display the beads and the drawings in the classroom so students may walk around and see what their classmates have done.

• Working in pairs, using beads and yarn, one student can start a pattern. The other student can continue the pattern.

• For second-grade students or advanced first-grade students, the teacher could address growing patterns.

Beads Everywhere!

Create a pattern. Ask a friend to finish it.

_____ created the pattern.

_____ finished the pattern.

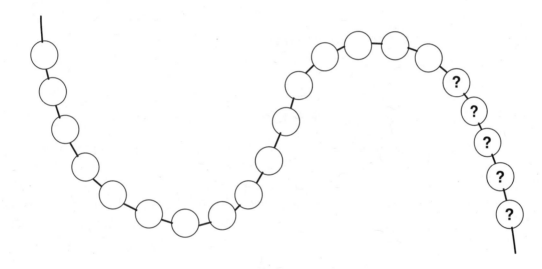

Describe the pattern you created. How is it the same or different from your partner's pattern?

Tell Its Trait

Grade-Level Band

PreK–2

Discussion of the Mathematics

In this lesson, students will identify common attributes of a set of blocks. The attributes include size (large and small), color (blue, red, yellow, and green), and shape (square, rectangle, triangle, circle, and pentagon). A one-circle Venn diagram will be used to sort the blocks. Students will be asked to identify the common attribute and add blocks to the Venn diagram that are the same size, color, or shape.

NCTM Standards

Algebra

- Sort and classify objects by size and other properties

Lesson Objectives

Upon successful completion of this lesson, the student will be able to:

- Sort blocks by size, color, and shape
- Identify common attributes of two or more blocks

Virtual Manipulatives Websites

National Library of Virtual Manipulatives for Interactive Math-
        ematics: http://nlvm.usu.edu/en/nav/vlibrary.html
Grade Band K–2, Geometry, Attribute Blocks:
        http://nlvm.usu.edu/en/nav/frames_asid_270_g_1_t_3.html?
        open=instructions

Materials

- A computer with an LCD projector for demonstration
- A computer with Internet connection for every two students
- "Tell Its Trait" activity sheet for each student
- Colored pencils, markers, or crayons

Mathematical Vocabulary

attribute, trait, square, rectangle, triangle, circle, pentagon

Activity and Teacher Notes

Approximate Duration of the Lesson
60 minutes

Warm-Up Discussion
Using an LCD projector and computer, go to the *National Library
of Virtual Manipulatives*. Click on the intersection of *Grade Band
Pre-K–2* and *Geometry*. Click on "Attribute Blocks." Ask students:
What do you notice about the blocks on the website? Try to elicit
the attribute and value words from students as you discuss what
they notice (size, color, shape, large, small, blue, red, yellow, green,
square, rectangle, triangle, circle, and pentagon). For example, if a
student says, "I see big shapes and little shapes," ask: When we use
the words "big" and "little," what characteristic of the blocks are
we describing? If a child says, "I see different colors," ask: What
colors do you see?

After discussing what the students notice about the blocks,
tell the students that size, shape, and color are *attributes* of the
blocks. Then review by asking: What sizes are there? What colors
are there? What shapes are there? Record the attributes and values on the blackboard or chart.

Teach the students how to name the blocks. Always say the size, then the color, then the shape (e.g., "a large green square").

Focus the students' attention on the shapes inside the oval (Venn diagram). "What is the same about all the blocks inside the oval?" Ask students to look for blocks on the outside of the oval that belong on the inside. "Tell a partner the name of a block that belongs on the inside of the oval." Have students tell you which blocks to move to the inside of the oval. Remind students to name the blocks correctly as they tell you which blocks to move.

After moving all the blocks that belong inside the oval, ask students, "What is the same about all the blocks inside the oval? What is different about the blocks inside the oval?" Then click on the Check button to check your work.

Click on the New Problem button to create a new problem. Have the class help you complete this problem in the same way as before.

Students Work with Partners

Have students work with partners to sort the virtual attribute blocks. Check students' understanding as they work. Ask questions such as, "What is the same about all the blocks in the Venn diagram? What do all those blocks have in common? Why doesn't the large blue square belong in that set? Does the small green triangle belong in the set? Why or why not?"

After students have worked on the website for 10–15 minutes, ask them to complete the activity sheet.

Teacher Tip

The first problem on the "Tell Its Trait" activity sheet is like the Website. It asks students to create a set with one common attribute. The second problem on the activity sheet is not like the Website. It asks students to create a set with two common attributes (e.g., blue squares). Students may need additional explanation to complete the second problem.

Follow-Up Discussion

Have students share the pictures of the sets they drew. Cover the descriptions of the sets with post-it notes before they share. Have the class guess the common attribute(s). Ask if there are any other blocks that would fit in the sets.

Student Assessment

- Can the student tell how two blocks are the same and/or different?
- Can the student identify the common attribute(s) of a set of blocks?
- Can the student tell why a given block fits (or does not fit) in a given set?

What to Expect from Students

Draw a set of blocks with two attributes in common.

The blocks in my set are the same ___*shape*___ and ___*color*___.

They are all ___*square*___ ___*green*___.

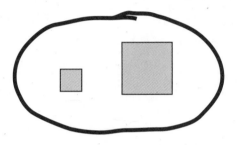

FIGURE 1. *Sample student work from the "Tell Its Trait" activity sheet.*

Extensions and Connections

Ask students to figure out how many different attribute blocks there are.

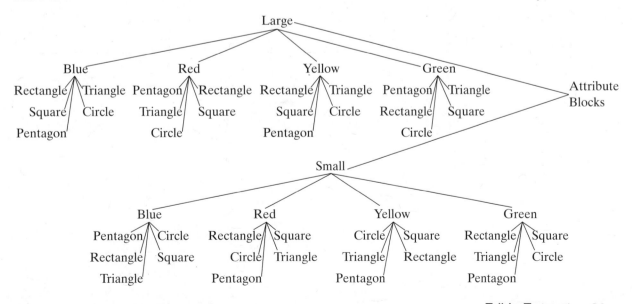

Tell Its Trait

Draw a set of blocks with one attribute in common.

The blocks in my set are all the same _____ (size, color, shape).

Draw a set of blocks with two attributes in common.

The blocks in my set are the same _____ and _____.

They are all _____ _____.

Patterns of Shapes

Grade-Level Band

3–5

Discussion of the Mathematics

In this lesson, students will use virtual pattern blocks to analyze patterns. The will be asked to generalize the patterns to the 100th term and the nth term. The patterns are set in a problem-solving context. If each side of a small square table can hold one seat, how many seats will there be when small tables are put together to form long, skinny tables?

NCTM Standards

Algebra

- Describe, extend, and make generalizations about geometric and numeric patterns
- Represent and analyze patterns and functions, using words, tables, and graphs

Lesson Objectives

Upon successful completion of this lesson, the student will be able to:

- Describe geometric and numeric patterns
- Represent patterns using pictures and charts
- Generalize patterns to the 100th and *n*th terms

Virtual Manipulatives Websites

National Library of Virtual Manipulatives for Interactive Mathematics: http://nlvm.usu.edu/en/nav/vlibrary.html

Grade Band 3–5, Algebra, Pattern Blocks: http://nlvm.usu.edu/en/nav/frames_asid_170_g_2_t_2.html?open=activities

Materials

- A computer with an LCD projector for demonstration
- A computer with Internet connection for every two students
- "Patterns of Shape" activity sheet for each group of students

Mathematical Vocabulary

pattern, term

Activity and Teacher Notes

Approximate Duration of the Lesson
60 minutes

Warm-Up Discussion
Go to the *National Library of Virtual Manipulatives*. Click on the intersection of *Grades 3–5* and *Algebra*. Click on "Pattern Blocks." Tell students that you have a problem that you would like them to solve: I have square tables that look like this. (Click on the square pattern block.) Say: Four people can sit at this square table. We'll use triangles to show the seats at the table. (Arrange 4 triangle pattern blocks around the square to show four seats at the table. See Figure 1.)

FIGURE I

Be sure to demonstrate how to rotate, move, and attach the virtual pattern blocks. Directions for these moves can be found by clicking on the teacher instructions for the applet. Make sure the students understand that each side of the square can hold only one seat.

Next, tell students that you have a long skinny room so you can only arrange the tables in a long row like this. (Show many square pattern blocks in a row. See Figure 2.) Tell students you are interested in finding out if there is a pattern that would help you figure out how many seats any given number of tables would hold.

FIGURE 2

Have students examine the chart on the "Patterns of Shape" activity sheet. Tell them you would like them to figure out the number of seats at tables made of 1 square, 2 squares, 3 squares, 4 squares, 5 squares, and 6 squares. They should use the virtual pattern blocks to figure out the answers, record the number of seats in the chart, and draw the arrangement they made using the virtual pattern blocks. Students should then analyze the chart, looking for a pattern that would help them figure out the number of seats at a table made of 100 square tables. The last question asks: "How could you determine the number of seats for any number of square tables?"

Students Work in Small Groups
Have students work with a partner or in groups of three. Guide them to the Pattern Blocks website. Circulate as they work on the problem. Ask questions such as: What patterns do you notice? How did you count the seats at the table? If I made a long table of 10 square tables, how many seats would there be? How do you know?

Follow-Up Discussion
Gather students in a common area. Review the answers on the "Patterns of Shape" activity sheet. Have students share their strategies for counting the number of seats at the long tables. (Some student may count the seats on the top and the seats on the bottom and then add the two end seats. Others may double the number of squares to determine the seats on the top and bottom and then add the two end seats. Both of these strategies are useful for determin-

ing the number of seats for any given table.) Ask students how they figured out the number of seats at a long table made of 100 small tables. Have students share their strategies for determining the number of seats for a table made of any number of square tables.

Student Assessment

- Can the student describe the pattern?
- Can the student generalize the pattern?
- Can the student write a formula for the pattern?
- Can the student explain how the formula works? (i.e., The triangular tables create a row with one seat for each triangle and a seat on each end. The square tables have two seats at each table plus one on each end of the row of tables.)
- Can the student generalize the rule for any regular polygon?

What to Expect from Students

- Students may initially assume that the number of seats is obtained by multiplying the number of tables by 4. Help students realize that seats are "lost" when tables are placed together in a skinny row.
- Students may attempt to make a prediction about the rule too early. Remind students that they should continue the pattern to make sure their rule works in every case.
- Students may not necessarily see the difference between the 100th term and the nth term. Remind students that n refers to any term—it's a general rule.

Extensions and Connections

Have students use virtual pattern blocks to find the number of seats at long tables made of triangular small tables or hexagonal small tables (use a clean copy of the "Patterns of Shapes" activity sheet).

Ask students to figure out the number of seats at tables made of octagonal or decagonal small tables.

Ask students to generalize the pattern to a polygon with 100 sides or any polygon.

Patterns of Shapes

There is a long, skinny room and square tables. One seat can fit on each side of a small square table. How many seats would there be if you put the small tables together in a long row?

# of Tables	# of Seats	Draw the Table Arrangement with the Seats
1		
2		
3		
4		
5		
6		
100		Tell how you know.

How could you determine the number of seats for any number of square tables?

Patterns of Shapes: Answer Keys

Answer Key – Square Tables

# of Tables	# of Seats	Arrangement
1	4	
2	6	
3	8	
4	10	
5	12	
6	15	
100	202	$2(100) + 2$
n	$2n + 2$	

Answer Key – Triangle Tables

# of Tables	# of Seats	Arrangement
1	3	
2	4	
3	5	
4	6	
5	7	
6	8	
100	102	$100 + 2$
n	$n + 2$	

Answer Key – Hexagon Tables

# of Tables	# of Seats	Arrangement
1	6	
2	10	
3	14	
4	18	
5	22	
6	26	
100	402	$4(100) + 2$
n	$4n + 2$	

Patterns of Shapes Activity (page 4)

Answer Key – Octagon Tables

# of Tables	# of Seats
1	8
2	14
3	20
4	26
5	32
6	48
100	602
n	$6n + 2$

Answer Key – Decagon Tables

# of Tables	# of Seats
1	10
2	18
3	26
4	34
5	42
6	50
100	802
n	$8n + 2$

Answer Key – Tables with 100 Sides

$98n + 2$

Answer Key – For Any Polygon

If s is the number of sides of the polygon and n is the number of tables in the arrangement, then the number of seats will be $(s - 2)(n) + 2$.

Come On Over to My Pad!

Grade-Level Band

6–8

Discussion of the Mathematics

When presented with a complex problem, students use a computer game to model and solve simpler versions of the problem. Students assemble the data they collect into a table in order to look for patterns and generalize a rule for solving the problem with any number.

NCTM Standards

Algebra

- Represent, analyze, and generalize a variety of patterns with tables, graphs, words, and, when possible, symbolic rules
- Model and solve contextualized problems using various representations, such as graphs, tables, and equations

Lesson Objectives

Upon successful completion of this lesson, the student will be able to:

- Solve a problem by creating a simpler problem
- Identify patterns found in data

Virtual Manipulatives Websites

National Library of Virtual Manipulatives for Interactive Mathematics: http://nlvm.usu.edu/en/nav/vlibrary.html

Grade Band 6–8, Algebra, Peg Puzzle:
http://nlvm.usu.edu/en/nav/frames_asid_182_g_3_t_2.html

Materials

- A computer with an LCD projector for demonstration
- A computer with Internet connection for every two students
- Transparency or poster of "Is the Lily Pad Greener on the Other Side of the Pond?" story
- "Come On Over to My Pad!" activity sheet for each student
- A red and a blue pencil for each student
- "Get Hopping" activity sheet for each student
- Large chart of table on "Get Hopping" activity sheet

Mathematical Vocabulary

pattern, formula, variable

Activity and Teacher Notes

Approximate Duration of the Lesson
Two 60-minute lessons

Day One
To introduce the problem, read "Is the Lily Pad Greener on the Other Side of the Pond?" story to the whole class (place copy on overhead). Call students' attention to the sentences in the story that tell how the frogs are situated (i.e., There were ten frogs in each group and there were twenty-one lily pads stretched across the pond. The lily pad in the middle always remained empty and the separate groups of frogs always remained on their side of the pond.) Ask students to use their own words to tell how the frogs are arranged (e.g., 12 lily pads in a straight line, 10 on one side, 10 on the other side, empty lily pad in the middle). Have volunteers repeat what they are being asked to do. Ask for a volunteer to draw a picture of the problem with just one pair of frogs on the board.

Explain to students that they will use a game on the computer to model the moves of the frogs. Using an LCD projector and computer with Internet connection, show students how to get to the website. Go the *National Library of Virtual Manipulatives*. Click on the intersection of *Grade Band 6–8* and *Algebra*. Then click on "Peg Puzzle." Hand out a copy of the "Come on Over to My Pad!" activity sheet to each student. Using the two-peg puzzle, model how to move the pegs and record the moves on the activity sheet using the red and blue pencils.

Have students work in pairs to solve the peg puzzles and complete the activity sheet. After most of the students have solved the problem with 2 pairs of pegs, but before they have solved the problem with 3 and 4 pairs of pegs, lead a class discussion. Ask students what they notice happening when they get stuck and what they notice happening when they are able to solve the problem. Students should notice that they get stuck when they put two of the same color together and that they solve the problem when they alternate colors. Allow students to continue working on the problem.

Day Two

Review the original problem and their experiences with the peg puzzle and place students in small groups. Hand out the "Get Hopping" activity sheet to each student. Have groups of students work together to complete the activity sheet with each student recording the information on his/her own sheet.

Bring the class together at the end of lesson for a whole-group discussion. Have students share the patterns they found. Have a large chart of the completed table so that students can refer to the data as they discuss the patterns. Ask if anyone created a formula that could determine the total number of moves for any number of frogs. Ask students to explain how the patterns helped them to develop their formulas. Try the formulas to see if they work.

Student Assessment

- Does the student recognize and describe various patterns in the data?
- Can the student identify rules or formulas for the patterns?
- Can the student generalize the pattern to the nth term?

What to Expect from Students

Recording the required moves is helpful to students in two ways. First it assists them in developing a strategy to successfully complete the peg game. Using the different colors and the different notation also helps students to see the patterns in the moves that lead to successful completion of the game. Once the moves are recorded, a variety of patterns can be seen.

The following pattern develops when students look at moves in the puzzle in terms of color. (Note that S = slide and J = jump.)

# pegs	Moves (# of moves)	Color Pattern
Two pegs	S J S (3)	1 red 1 blue 1 red
Four pegs	S J S J J S J S (8)	1 red 2 blue 2 red 2 blue 1 red
Six pegs	S J S J J S J J J S J J S J S (15)	1 red 2 blue 3 red 3 blue 3 red 2 blue 1 red
Eight pegs	S J S J J S J J J S J J J J S J J J S J J S J S (24)	1 red 2 blue 3 red 4 blue 4 red 4 blue 3 red 2 blue 1 red

The following pattern develops when students look at moves in the puzzle in terms of type of move (slide or jump):

Number of pegs	Moves	Pattern of Moves
Two pegs	S J S	1 1 1
Four pegs	S J S J J S J S	1 1 1 2 1 1 1
Six pegs	S J S J J S J J J S J J S J S	1 1 1 2 1 3 1 2 1 1 1
Eight pegs	S J S J J S J J J S J J J J S J J J S J J S J S	1 1 1 2 1 3 1 4 1 3 1 2 1 1 1

In order to successfully complete the table, the students will need to discover the patterns in the various rows and columns. The completed table is shown below:

Pairs of Frogs	Number of Slides	Number of Jumps	Total # of Moves
1	2	1	3
2	4	4	8
3	6	9	15
4	8	16	24
5	10	25	35
6	12	36	48
7	14	49	63
8	16	64	80
9	18	81	99
10	20	100	120

Students will discover a variety of patterns, including some or all of the following:

- Slides plus jumps equal total moves
- The slide column is increasing by two each time
- The jump column increases by 3, then 5, then 7, . . . (adding two more each time)
- The total move column increases by 5, then 7, then 9, . . . (adding two more each time)
- The number of slides equals the number of pairs of frogs times 2 (or $2n$)
- The number of jumps equals the number of pairs of frogs times itself (or n^2)

Students may discover several formulas for the final column including:

- Using the patterns from above: $2n + n^2$
- Observing that the total number of moves can be obtained by adding two to the number of pairs of frogs and then multiplying that number by the number of pairs of frogs: $(n + 2) \times n$
- They may notice that the total number of moves is one less than the number of pairs plus one squared: $(n + 1)^2 - 1$

The table allows the students to organize their data in a way that helps to lead them to discover many different patterns. If desired, the "Get Hopping" worksheet can be omitted and students could be directed to organize their data in some way that will assist them in finding the number of moves for ten pairs of frogs. In this instance, groups are likely to focus on some of the patterns that lead them to solve the problem. During the whole-group discussion, comparisons may be made among successful strategies, stressing the different ways available to solve the same problem.

Extensions and Connections
- Students could explore events that exhibit similar patterns
- Students could create story problems that would fit the pattern discovered

References

Maletsky, E., and M. K. Varley. 2004. *Building Big Ideas*. Rowley, MA: Didax, Inc.

Is the Lily Pad Greener on the Other Side of the Pond?

Once upon a time, on a pond far, far away, there lived two groups of frogs. The Croaks (as they preferred to be called) were a beautiful shade of green and they lived on the left side of the pond. The Bits (for "Rib-bit") lived on the right side of the pond and were a pale shade of brown with iridescent blue dots. Most of their time was spent sitting on the lily pads out in the pond. There were ten frogs in each group, and there were twenty-one lily pads stretched across the pond. The lily pad in the middle always remained empty, and the separate groups of frogs always remained on their side of the pond.

One day, a member of the Croaks looked across the pond and thought, "I think the lily pads on the other side of the pond look greener than our side. I bet we would look even better if we were sitting on them." As fate would have it, at the same moment, a member of the Bits was observing that the lily pads on the side of the pond opposite from where his group sat appeared to be a darker shade of green that day. He thought to himself, "I bet our shimmering blue dots would really stand out if we were sitting on those lily pads." After a quick discussion within each group, the two groups of frogs decided to switch sides of the pond, but they were concerned about how much time and effort this activity might take. While this might seem like an easy thing to do, proper frog etiquette must always be followed when moving on lily pads. The only way the frogs can switch places is to slide forward onto an empty lily pad or to jump over another frog.

Can you help the Croaks and the Bits determine how many slides and jumps will be needed? In other words, how many moves will it take for the two groups to switch places on the pond?

And then will they live happily ever?????

Come On Over to My Pad!

Play the Peg Puzzle game until you have been successful at each level several times. Record your moves in the spaces provided below. Use red and blue colored pencils to show when you moved a red or blue peg. Record your moves as red or blue S's (for slides) and J's (for jumps). Example: S (red) J (blue) J (blue) means you slid a red peg, then jumped with a blue peg, then jumped with a blue peg.

Two pegs (one pair of frogs):

Record moves:

Number of moves required: _____

Four pegs (two pairs of frogs):

Record moves:

Number of moves required: _____

Six pegs (three pairs of frogs):

Record moves:

Number of moves required: _____

Eight pegs (four pairs of frogs):

Record moves:

Number of moves required: _____

Get Hopping

Group Members: _____

Using the data you gathered during the peg game, complete the table below for 1–4 pairs of frogs. Look for patterns in the table in order to help you complete the table for 10 pairs of frogs.

Pairs of Frogs	Number of Slides	Number of Jumps	Total # of Moves
1			
2			
3			
4			
5			
6			
7			
8			
9			
10			

1. Describe all the patterns you found in the data in the table above. Use the back of this page if needed.

2. Explain how you determined the total number of moves required for 10 pairs of frogs. Use the back of this page if needed.

Sample Lesson 8: Geometry

Copycat

Grade-Level Band

PreK–2

Discussion of the Mathematics

In this lesson, students explore combining pattern block shapes to cover larger shapes. They manipulate virtual pattern blocks using transformations (slides and turns).

NCTM Standards

Geometry
- Investigate and predict the results of putting together and taking apart two-dimensional shapes
- Describe, name, and interpret relative positions in space and apply ideas about relative position
- Recognize and apply slides, flips, and turns
- Create mental images of geometric shapes using spatial memory and spatial visualization

Lesson Objectives

Upon successful completion of this lesson, the student will be able to:
- Put pattern blocks together to create new shapes
- Describe transformations of virtual pattern blocks using the terms *slide* and *turn*

Virtual Manipulatives Websites

National Library of Virtual Manipulatives for Interactive Mathematics: http://nlvm.usu.edu/en/nav/vlibrary.html
Grade Band PreK–2, Geometry, Pattern Blocks:
http://nlvm.usu.edu/en/nav/frames_asid_169_g_1_t_3.html

Materials

- A computer with an LCD projector for demonstration
- A computer with Internet connection for every two students
- "Copycat Activity Sheet 1" for each student
- "Copycat Activity Sheet 2" for each student

Mathematical Vocabulary

shape, hexagon, trapezoid, rhombus, triangle, square, slide, turn

Activity and Teacher Notes

Approximate Duration of the Lesson
60 minutes

Warm-Up Discussion
Using an LCD projector and computer with Internet access, go to the *National Library of Virtual Manipulatives*. Click on the intersection of *Grade Band Pre-K–2* and *Geometry*. Then click on "Pattern Blocks." Show students how to add a block to the workspace. As you add the blocks to the workspace, have students describe the shapes by naming them, counting the sides and angles, and comparing the sizes.

Show students how to rotate a block, change the color of a block, remove a block from the workspace, group blocks, clone blocks, zoom in and out, and clear the workspace. (Directions can be found by clicking on the Instructions button.)

Model the Activity
Model the first problem on Activity Sheet 1. Select the shapes in column 1 (hexagon) and column 2 (two trapezoids). Then manipulate the trapezoids to cover the hexagon. Have students describe the movements (slide or turn) as you do it. Tell students they will do the rest of the problems on Activity Sheet 1 with a partner.

Ask if anyone can think of another way to cover the hexagon. Model one of the student's suggestions. Tell students that they will find as many ways as they can to cover the hexagon and record the ways on Activity Sheet 2.

Students Work with Partners

Have students work together to complete Activity Sheets 1 and 2. The students should take turns operating the virtual manipulatives. The student who is not manipulating the virtual pattern blocks should orally describe the moves that the other student is making. Both students should record their answers on the activity sheets.

Follow-Up Discussion

Have students share the different ways they found to cover the hexagon and the large triangle. Students should verbally describe the transformations as you manipulate the blocks to cover the hexagon. (See Answer Key for all the ways.)

Student Assessment

- Can the student put pattern blocks together to cover other pattern blocks?
- Can the student verbally describe the transformations (slides and turns) used to maneuver the pattern blocks?
- Can the student find multiple ways to cover the hexagon?
- Can the student find multiple ways to create a large triangle?
- Can the student predict (visualize) which pattern blocks will cover another?

What to Expect from Students

The following answer keys provide all possible answers for the problems on Activity Sheet 2.

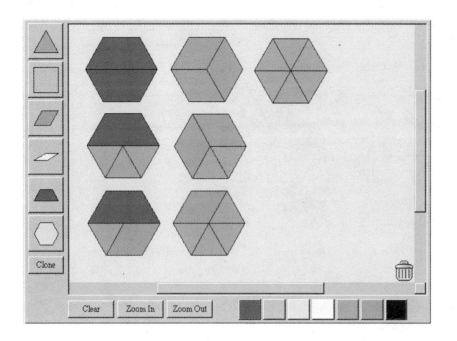

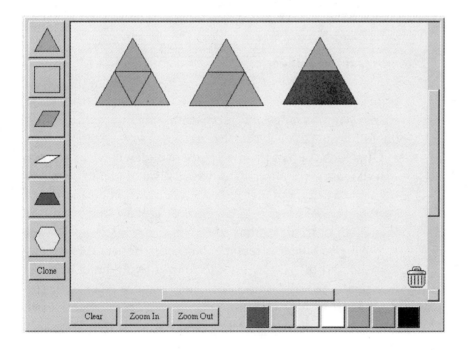

Sample student work on the activity sheet is shown below.

Find as many ways as you can to cover the hexagon.

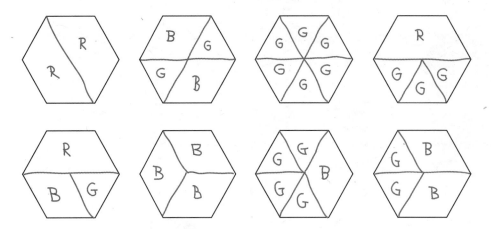

Extensions and Connections

1. Prior to the lesson, students need experience visualizing shapes within shapes and representing them graphically. Try the following paper-folding exercises.
   - Give each student a square piece of paper. Have her or him fold the square into halves diagonally and identify the new shape created (triangle). Ask students to open the paper, trace the fold line with a pencil or crayon, and count the number of triangles they see.
   - Next, give students rectangular pieces of paper. Have students fold the rectangles into fourths by folding the paper in half vertically and in half horizontally. Again ask students to identify the new shape (smaller rectangle), open the sheet, trace the fold lines, and count the new shapes.
2. Tell students that sometimes they need to look at objects very closely to find the shapes inside of them. Tell students they will be looking for shapes inside of other shapes as you read the story, *Three Pigs, One Wolf, and Seven Magic Shapes* by Grace Maccarone. After reading the book, give each student a set of tangram pieces. Have partners work together to solve the fol-

lowing problems (Note: Each pair of students must have two complete sets of tangram pieces to do the activities.):

- Use 2 large triangles to make a square.
- Use 2 small squares to make a rectangle.
- Use 4 small triangles to make a square.
- Use 2 triangles and a square to make a trapezoid.

Copycat
Activity Sheet 1

Cover this shape:	With this:
1.	
2.	
3.	
4.	
5.	
6. Use 2 or 3 pattern blocks to create your own shape.	Which blocks did you use?

Copycat
Activity Sheet 2

Directions: Use pattern blocks to make the shapes below. Draw the pattern blocks you used on each shape.

Find as many ways as you can to cover the hexagon.

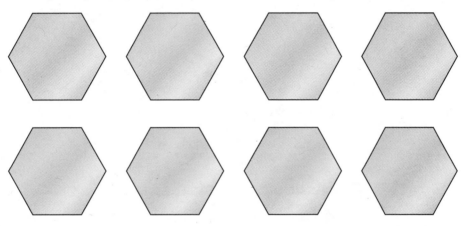

Find as many ways as you can to combine triangles to make a larger triangle.

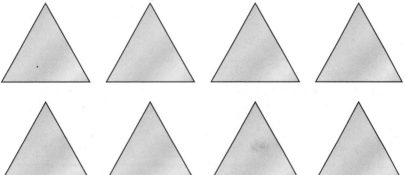

Constructing Shapes

Grade-Level Band

3–5

Discussion of the Mathematics

In this lesson, students will use virtual geoboards to create polygons. The virtual geoboard will compute the area and perimeter of the shapes. Students will learn that different shapes can have the same area or perimeter. Students should have experience computing perimeter and area of plane figures using graph paper, concrete manipulatives, and real world objects prior to this lesson.

NCTM Standards

Geometry

- Build and draw geometric objects
- Use geometric models to solve problems in other areas of mathematics, such as number and measurement

Measurement
- Understand such attributes as length and area and select the appropriate type of unit for measuring each attribute
- Explore what happens to measurements of a two-dimensional shape such as its perimeter and area when the shape is changed in some way

Lesson Objectives

Upon successful completion of this lesson, the student will be able to:
- Create plane figures with given dimensions
- Understand perimeter and area
- Solve problems involving perimeter and area

Virtual Manipulatives Websites

National Library of Virtual Manipulatives for Interactive Mathematics: http://nlvm.usu.edu/en/nav/vlibrary.html

Grade Band 3–5, Geometry, Geoboard: http://nlvm.usu.edu/en/nav/frames_asid_172_g_2_t_3.html? open=activities

Materials

- A computer with an LCD projector for demonstration
- A computer with Internet connection for every two students
- "Constructing Shapes" activity sheet for each student

Mathematical Vocabulary

area, perimeter, length, width, polygon, unit, square unit, square, rectangle, triangle

Activity and Teacher Notes

Approximate Duration of the Lesson
60 minutes

Warm-Up Discussion
Go to the *National Library of Virtual Manipulatives*. Click on the intersection of *Grade Band 3–5* and *Geometry*. Click on "Geoboard." Explain to students that the space between two pegs on a geoboard is one unit. Model how to connect a virtual rubber band between two pegs. Illustrate how to draw the line on geodot paper. Tell students that a square that measures one unit on each side is a square unit. Model how to form a square unit on the virtual geoboard using one rubber band. Click on Measures to show the area and perimeter of the shape.

Teacher Tip

A shape must be formed by one rubber band for the computer to calculate its dimensions. Model how to draw the square on geodot paper. Hand out the "Constructing Shapes" activity sheet to each student, and point out the information that you just discussed in the Getting Started section.

Do the "Explore" section of the activity sheet with the students. Using an LCD projector, call on students to create each of the polygons for the class. Be sure the area and perimeter measures are hidden. Have students give the area and perimeter of each shape that is created and explain their strategies for finding them.

Students Work Independently

Have students work independently to complete the "You Do the Math" section of the "Constructing Shapes" activity sheet. Guide students to the virtual geoboards website. Give students a few minutes to explore the virtual geoboard, and then have students complete the activities on the activity sheet. Students should record the polygons they create on geodot paper.

Follow-Up Discussion

Once students have completed the activity sheet, select several students to share their responses on large dot paper. Display student responses for each problem separately so the class can see multiple solutions to the problems. Use the following questions to lead a discussion.

Which shapes did you create that had a perimeter of 16 units? What strategies did you use to keep the areas the same while changing the perimeters (problems b, c, and d)? Compare the polygons for problems b, c, and d. What do you notice about the shapes as the perimeters get smaller? (The more compact the polygon is, the fewer sides there are to "walk around.")

Student Assessment

- Can the student create a shape with the given dimensions?
- Does the student have strategies for changing the perimeter of a shape while the area remains constant?
- Does the student have strategies for changing the area of a shape while the perimeter remains constant?
- Can the student explain what *area* means?
- Can the student explain what *perimeter* means?

What to Expect from Students

- Many students will use a guess-and-check strategy to solve the problems. This is acceptable and still allows children to see that different shapes can have the same area or perimeter. In discussion, encourage students to explain why different shapes have equal or unequal dimensions.
- Constructing triangles will present a problem for the students. It is not an indication of failure if students do not solve these problem types. Rather, the triangle problems are included to challenge the thinking of advanced students.

Extensions and Connections

Ask students to respond to one or more of the following journal prompts:

1. Can you increase the perimeter of a polygon without increasing its area? Why or why not? *Yes, because you can join each square unit to the others so that only one of its sides is hidden (not part of the perimeter).*
2. I have 6 square tables in my classroom. Only one student can sit at each side of a table. If at least one side of each table must be touching one side of another table, how can I arrange the tables to seat the most students?
3. Given area = 8 square units, find the polygon with the greatest perimeter. How do you know this polygon has the greatest perimeter? *A "stretched" rectangle with length (or width) of 1 unit.*
4. How can you find the area of a triangle? *A triangle is one-half of a rectangle with the same length and width.*

Name _____ Date _____

Constructing Shapes

Getting Started

The space between two pegs on a geoboard is one unit.

A square that measures one unit on each side is a square unit (sq unit).

Make a square unit on the geoboard.

Explore

1. Use one rubber band to create each of the following polygons on the computer geoboard.

2. Find the perimeter and area of each shape by clicking on the button marked *Measures*.

   a) a rectangle with an area of 3 square units

   b) a square with length 2 units and width 2 units

   c) triangle with length 2 units and width 2 units

   d) a polygon shaped like an L

   e) a polygon with 5 sides

You Do the Math

1. Use your computer geoboard to create shapes with the measurements below. Use one rubber band for each polygon.

2. Check the perimeter and area by clicking on *Measures*.

3. Copy the polygon on the geodot paper.

   a) perimeter – 16 units, area – 16 square units

   b) perimeter – 12 units, area – 9 sq units

   c) perimeter – 16 units, area – 9 sq units

   d) perimeter – 20 units, area – 9 sq units

   e) perimeter – 14 units, area – 10 sq units

   f) triangle, area – 5 sq units

   g) triangle, area – 8 sq units

Constructing Shapes Activity

perimeter = _____ units

area = _____ sq units

perimeter = _____ units

area = _____ sq units

Tangrams

Grade-Level Band

3–5

Discussion of the Mathematics

In this lesson, students will use visualization, spatial reasoning, and geometric reasoning to solve tangram puzzles. The puzzles involve combining two-dimensional shapes to cover larger two-dimensional shapes. Students will use transformations (slides, flips, and turns) to maneuver virtual tangram pieces to solve the puzzles. They will also build their mathematical vocabulary by making predictions and describing the transformations they use.

NCTM Standards

Geometry

- Investigate, describe, and reason about the results of subdividing, combining, and transforming shapes
- Describe location and movement using common language and geometric vocabulary
- Predict and describe the results of sliding, flipping, and turning two-dimensional shapes

Lesson Objectives

Upon successful completion of this lesson, the student will be able to:

- Combine tangram pieces (two-dimensional shapes) to form new shapes
- Describe transformations as slides, flips, and turns
- Predict the results of sliding, flipping, and turning tangram pieces (two-dimensional shapes)

Virtual Manipulatives Websites

National Library of Virtual Manipulatives for Interactive Mathematics: http://nlvm.usu.edu/en/nav/vlibrary.html

Grade Band 3–5, Geometry, Tangrams: http://nlvm.usu.edu/en/nav/frames_asid_289_g_2_t_3.html? open=activities

Materials

- A computer with an LCD projector for demonstration
- A computer with Internet connection for every two students
- Tangram template printed on colored paper (optional)
- Scissors (optional)
- Blank white paper (optional)

Mathematical Vocabulary

tangram, triangle, parallelogram, square, slide, flip, turn, transformation, rotate

Activity and Teacher Notes

Approximate Duration of the Lesson
60 minutes

Warm-Up Discussion
Go to the *National Library of Virtual Manipulatives*. Click on the intersection of *Grades 3–5* and *Geometry*. Click on "Tangrams." Show students how to move, rotate, and flip the virtual blocks, how

to change the color of the blocks, and how to reset the workspace. (Directions can be found by clicking on the Instructions button.)

Click on one of the gray shapes at the bottom of the page. Have students tell you how to move the tangram pieces to cover the gray shape. Have them use words such as *slide*, *flip*, and *turn* to describe the moves as you make them. Tell students that they will be doing the same activity at their own computers.

Students Work with Partners

Have students work with a partner to do the activity. Partners should take turns manipulating the shapes and verbally directing the movements. (One student tells the other student how to move the shapes.) They should try as many of the gray shapes as time allows. Observe students as they work. Listen to the language they are using to describe the transformation of the shapes. Check for understanding. Provide assistance as needed.

Follow-Up Discussion

In a discussion with the whole class, ask students what was easy/ hard about doing the tangram puzzles. What strategies did they use? Which puzzle did they think was the hardest? Which was the easiest? Why?

Student Assessment

- Can the student combine tangram pieces to cover the gray shapes?
- Can the student name the types of transformations (slides, flips, turns) he/she is using to maneuver the tangram pieces?
- Can the student visualize how the tangram pieces will fit together to cover a gray shape?
- Can the student describe/predict how the shape will be transformed before doing it?

What to Expect from Students

- Students may create a tangram puzzle in which pieces are located outside the confines of the perimeter, as shown below.

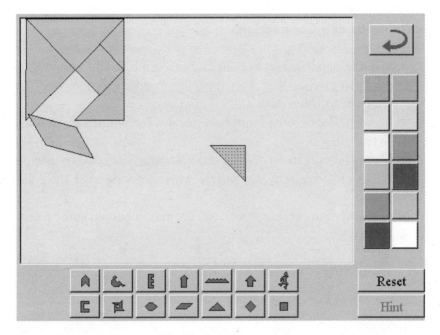

- Students may create a tangram puzzle in which pieces are overlapping, as shown below.

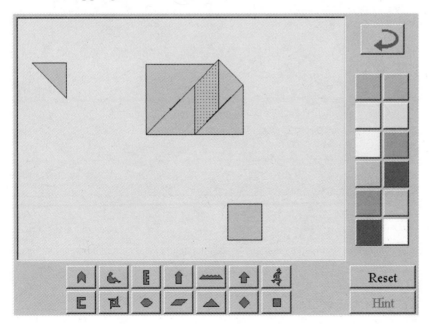

- Students may create a tangram puzzle in which a small piece is uncovered, and no tangram pieces fit in that spot.

In each of these cases, consider how you will guide students to correct their mistakes.

Extensions and Connections

- Use the paper tangram template (shown below) to allow students to create their own tangram puzzle. Provide time for students to solve each others' puzzles.
- Have students create tangram puzzles for parents or siblings to try at home.
- Have students discuss/write the vocabulary needed to discuss how to solve a tangram puzzle with someone over the telephone.
- Have students create directions for making and solving a tangram puzzle.

Building with Space Blocks

Grade-Level Band

6–8

Discussion of the Mathematics

In this lesson, students will use visualization and spatial reasoning to solve problems involving surface area of solid shapes. They will build geometric solids with cubes using space blocks (a virtual manipulative). It is recommended that actual cubes are also available (centimeter cubes, 2-cm cubes, or inch cubes) as some students may have difficulty visualizing three-dimensional figures on a two-dimensional computer screen.

Student will be asked to solve three problems using the space blocks:

1. Connect 8 blocks to form a solid with the smallest possible surface area.
2. Connect 8 blocks to form a solid with the largest possible surface area.
3. Connect 8 blocks to form a solid with surface area equal to 28 square units.

Students will also be asked to write similar problems involving surface area. They will use isometric dot paper to draw their solutions. They will explain their strategies for solving the problems and finding surface area. Students will work with partners as they solve problems and share solution strategies.

In this activity students will build rectangular prisms and other solid shapes. Encourage students to find the surface area of all the shapes they create, but pay particular attention to the rectangular prisms. Encourage students to develop procedures and formulas for finding the surface area of a rectangular prism.

NCTM Standards

Geometry
- Use two-dimensional representations of three-dimensional objects to visualize and solve problems such as those involving surface area and volume

Measurement
- Understand, select, and use units of appropriate size and type to measure surface area and volume
- Develop strategies to determine the surface area and volume of selected prisms

Lesson Objectives

Upon successful completion of this lesson, the student will be able to:

- Investigate and solve problems involving the surface area of solid shapes
- Use visualization, spatial reasoning, and geometric modeling to solve problems
- Develop a procedure and formula for finding the surface area of a rectangular prism

Virtual Manipulatives Websites

National Library of Virtual Manipulatives for Interactive Mathematics: http://nlvm.usu.edu/en/nav/vlibrary.html
Grade Band 6–8, Geometry, Space Blocks:
http://nlvm.usu.edu/en/nav/frames_asid_195_g_3_t_3.html?
open=activities

Materials

- A computer with an LCD projector for demonstration
- A computer with Internet connection for every two students
- "Building with Space Blocks" activity sheet for each student
- Wooden cubes (optional)

Mathematical Vocabulary

surface area, cube, rectangular prism, face, edge, vertex, minimum, maximum, base

Activity and Teacher Notes

Approximate Duration of the Lesson
60 minutes

Warm-Up Discussion
Go to the *National Library of Virtual Manipulatives*. Click on the intersection of *Grade Band 6–8* and *Geometry*. Click on "Space Blocks." Model the Space Blocks website for students. Show them how to add blocks, turn blocks, and connect blocks.

Give each student a "Space Blocks" activity sheet.

Teacher Tip
The three problems posed in this lesson are on the Space Blocks website. Click on Activities. In the Activities section on the right, click on the left or right arrows to select from the available activity choices. Students will work on the problem "Minimizing Surface Area" first, the problem "Maximizing Surface Area" second, and the problem "Constructing Figures with a Given Surface Area" third.

Explain the activity, showing students how to locate the three problems on the website and how to check their solutions. Review the concept of *surface area* by asking students to figure out the surface area of a shape that you have created on the Space Blocks website. (Do not create a shape that solves one of the problems posed on the site.) Tell students that they may work together, but each student must fill out his or her own activity sheet. Model how to draw using isometric dot paper.

Teacher Tip

Students will also create their own problems. When they create their own problems, they can use the website to build solid shapes, but the computer will not check their work. Be sure they understand this aspect of the website.

Students Work with Partners

Allow students time to complete the activity sheet. Students should work with a partner. Encourage partners to solve each others' problems and discuss their solution strategies. Circulate as students are working. Ask: How do you know when you've found the minimum surface area? Why do you think the shape you created has the largest surface area? What is your strategy for building a solid with a surface area of 28 square units?

Follow-Up Discussion

Ask students to share their solution strategies. Focus on strategies for finding the surface area of rectangular prisms. Ask students to explain their strategies for finding the solid shape with the least amount of surface area, the greatest amount of surface area, and a given amount of surface area. Ask students if they have a rule for figuring out the surface area of any given rectangular prism.

Teacher Tip

The surface area of a rectangular prism is the sum of the areas of all six faces (SA = $2lw + 2lh + 2wh$).

Student Assessment

- Does the student use appropriate vocabulary such as *surface area*, *cube*, *rectangular prism*, *face*, *edge*, and *vertex*?
- Can the student explain his or her strategies for building solid shapes with minimum, maximum, and given surface areas? (The shapes may or may not be rectangular prisms.)
- Can the student find the surface area of a given rectangular solid? Can the student explain his/her procedure for finding the surface area?
- Can the student articulate a formula for finding the surface area of a cube?
- Can the student articulate a formula for finding the surface area of a rectangular prism that is not a cube?

What to Expect from Students

Sample student work from the "Building Shapes" activity sheet is shown below. (These images represent two possible responses to Question 2 on the activity sheet.)

Maximum Surface Area

2. Connect 8 blocks to form a solid with the largest possible surface area. Draw your solid shape below. What is the surface area of this solid shape? _____34_____

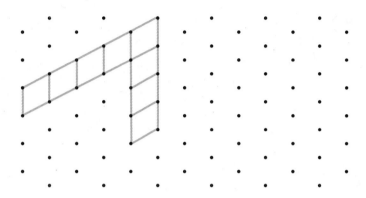

Maximum Surface Area

2. Connect 8 blocks to form a solid with the largest possible surface area. Draw your solid shape below. What is the surface area of this solid shape? _____34_____

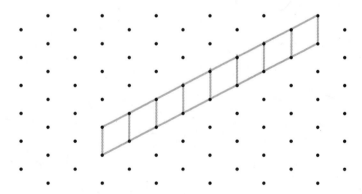

Extensions and Connections

- Using the Space Blocks website, have students find all the possible arrangements using five cubes and calculate the surface area of each arrangement.
- Have students use the concepts from this lesson to configure houses based on various prices for the foundation, roof, and walls. Students could research the costs of each of these (e. g., a foundation might cost more than a wall) and configure houses to certain specifications.

Building with Space Blocks

Minimizing Surface Area

1. Connect 8 blocks to form a solid with the smallest possible surface area. Draw your solid shape below. What is the surface area of this solid shape? _____

_____

Maximizing Surface Area

2. Connect 8 blocks to form a solid with the largest possible surface area. Draw your solid shape below. What is the surface area of this solid shape? _____

_____

Constructing Figures with a Given Surface Area

3. Connect 8 blocks to form a solid with a surface area equal to 28 square units.
    Draw your solid shape below.

4. What strategies did you use to figure out the surface areas of solid shapes?

_____

_____

_____

_____

_____

_____

_____

_____

Write your own surface area problems. Ask a friend to use space blocks to figure out the answers to your problems. Write your problems below.

5. _____

_____

_____

6. _____

_____

_____

Sample Lesson 12:
Data Analysis & Probability

Spinning, Spinning: Where It Lands, No One Knows

Grade-Level Band

PreK–2

Discussion of the Mathematics

In this lesson, students will spin a five-color spinner 20 times and record the results of the spins in a tally chart. They will compare their results to a bar graph created by the computer program. Students will then create a large bar graph of the class results using Unifix cubes. The class results will be analyzed and discussed.

NCTM Standards

Data Analysis and Probability

- Represent data using pictures and graphs
- Describe parts of the data and the set of data as a whole to determine what the data show
- Discuss events related to students' experiences as likely or unlikely

Lesson Objectives

Upon successful completion of this lesson, the student will be able to:

- Predict the probability of outcomes of simple experiments using spinners and test the predictions
- Represent and interpret data using tally marks
- Compare and contrast data represented by tally marks with data represented on bar graphs

Virtual Manipulatives Websites

National Library of Virtual Manipulatives for Interactive Mathematics: http://nlvm.usu.edu/en/nav/vlibrary.html

Grade Band Pre-K–2, Data Analysis & Probability, Spinners: http://nlvm.usu.edu/en/nav/frames_asid_186_g_1_t_5.html?open=activities

Materials

- A computer with Internet connection for every two students
- "Spinning, Spinning: Where It Lands No One Knows" activity sheet for each pair of students
- Unifix cubes (approximately 75 cubes of each color: red, orange, yellow, green, blue)

Mathematical Vocabulary

probability, chance, likely, unlikely, possible, impossible, bar graph

Activity and Teacher Notes

Approximate Duration of the Lesson

60 minutes

Warm-Up Discussion

Present the five-colored spinner on the website to the class and ask what colors the spinner could land on if it were spun. Ask: What colors would be impossible to land on? Ask: If we spun the spinner 10 times, how many times do you think it would land on red? Why do you think so?

Model the Activity

Show students how to spin the virtual spinner and model how to record tally marks on the activity sheet. Show students how to click on Record Results to see the bar graph. Tell them you would like them to write how the tally marks are the same and different from the bar graph on their activity sheet.

Students Work with Partners

Have students work with a partner using the virtual spinner. Ask students to spin the spinner 20 times and record the results on the student activity sheet.

Teacher Tip

You can increase or decrease the number of colors on the spinner to differentiate instruction for more advanced or struggling students.

With each spin, students should cross out one of the numbers on the bottom of the page to keep track of how many times they have spun the spinner.

Teacher Tip

Expect that at first students will have some difficulty working the spinner program on the website.

Ask students to compare the results on their tally chart to the bar graph produced by the computer program.

As students work, circulate and ask questions. How many spins have landed on red, blue, etc.? What color do you think the spinner will land on next? Why do you think so? Which color has the spinner landed on the most (the least)? How is the bar graph the same (different) from the tally chart?

Follow-Up Discussion

When the students have finished their 20 spins, ask them to take a Unifix cube for each of their 20 tally marks. The color of the Unifix cubes should match the colors that were spun on their spinners. Since there is no purple Unifix cube, have the students use blue cubes to represent purple spins. Have students stack the Unifix cubes by color and then bring the students together as a class. Combine the Unifix cubes by color to make a large bar graph of the class results. You might stand the stacks up on the chalk tray or lay them on the floor where all the students can see them.

Ask: What color was landed on the most? The least? If we were to spin again, which color do you think the spinner would land on? Why? Is it possible if we spin again we will land on (choose any color here)? Why or why not?

Teacher Tip

When discussing the results, students may expect the spinner to land on the color that was landed on the most. It is important that they realize there is an equal chance of landing on any of the five colors each time they spin.

Student Assessment

- Does the student make reasonable predictions?
- Does the student use tally marks correctly?
- How does the student count the tally marks? By tens and ones? By fives and ones? By ones only?

What to Expect from Students

A sample bar graph, as shown on a computer screen, is pictured below.

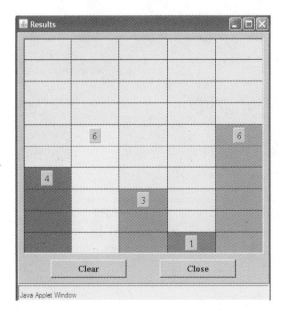

Extensions and Connections

Ask students if they think they would get the same results if they did the experiment again. Have the students clear the graph. Using a new activity sheet, have the students repeat the activity. Discuss the similarities and differences between the two experiments.

Name _____   Date _____

Spinning, Spinning: Where It Lands, No One Knows

Tally Chart

RED	ORANGE	YELLOW	GREEN	PURPLE

1   2   3   4   5   6   7   8   9   10
11 12 13 14 15 16 17 18 19 20

Compare your tally marks to the bar graph.

What is the same?

What is different?

Spinning, Spinning: Where It Lands, No One Knows Activity

Secret Spinners

Grade-Level Band

3–5

Discussion of the Mathematics

In this lesson, students explore probability by creating virtual spinners and conducting probability experiments with those spinners. Working in small groups, students create virtual spinners with given criteria. The configurations of the spinners are kept hidden from the other groups. The students conduct probability experiments with the secret spinners and record the results on bar graphs. At the end of the lesson, the bar graphs are posted, and students are asked to match the secret spinners to the bar graphs. As students match the spinners to the graphs, they justify and explain their decisions based upon their knowledge of probability. Students also have opportunities to discuss the difference between theoretical and experimental probability, as some of the experiments may not yield the expected results. They may notice that the experimental probability approaches the theoretical probability as the number of spins increases.

NCTM Standards

Data Analysis and Probability

- Collect data using observations, surveys, and experiments

- Represent data using tables and graphs such as bar graphs
- Describe events as likely or unlikely and discuss the degree of likelihood using such words as *certain, equally likely,* and *impossible*
- Understand that the measure of the likelihood of an event can be represented by a number from 0 to 1

Lesson Objectives

Upon successful completion of this lesson, the student will be able to:

- Design a spinner based on given criteria
- Predict the outcomes of simple experiments using spinners and test the predictions
- Determine the probability of a given simple event
- Write probability as ratios
- Represent and interpret data using bar graphs

Virtual Manipulatives Websites

National Library of Virtual Manipulatives for Interactive Mathematics: http://nlvm.usu.edu/en/nav/vlibrary.html

Grade Band 3–5, Data Analysis & Probability, Spinner: http://nlvm.usu.edu/en/nav/frames_asid_186_g_2_t_5.html?open=activities

Materials

- A computer with an LCD projector for demonstration
- A computer with Internet connection for each group of students
- 1 copy of Secret Spinner Cards (cut apart)
- 9" × 12" envelopes (one for each group)
- Secret Spinner Record Sheets (one for each group)
- Bar Graph Templates (one for each group)
- Large Spinner Templates (one for each group)
- Markers (set of 8 classic colors for each group)
- Secret Spinner Class Summary Page (one for each student)

Mathematical Vocabulary

probability, outcome, chance, multiple, factor, fraction, ratio, likely, unlikely, equally likely, possible, impossible, likelihood

Activity and Teacher Notes

Preparation

1. Divide the class into 6–12 groups of 2–4 students. Each group will need a computer with Internet access.
2. Prepare a Secret Spinner envelope for each group. Each envelope should contain:
   - A Secret Spinner Card (a different card for each group)
   - A Secret Spinner Record Sheet
   - A Bar Graph Template
   - A Spinner Template

Approximate Duration of the Lesson

60 minutes

Warm-Up Discussion

Using an LCD projector and computer with Internet connection, go to the *National Library of Virtual Manipulatives*. Click on the intersection of *Grade Band 3–5* and *Data Analysis & Probability*. Then click on "Spinner." Use the virtual spinner to create a spinner that is half green and half yellow.

Ask: What is the likelihood that the arrow will land on green when I spin this spinner? (Students should explain that there is an equal chance of getting green or yellow.) Ask: What fraction would describe the probability of landing on green?

Ask: How could I design a spinner that has a greater chance of landing on green than yellow? Elicit student responses and then create a spinner based upon the recommendation of one of the students. Ask: What is the probability of landing on green? Write the probability in the form of a fraction.

Explore spinning the spinner. First click on the Record Results button to turn on the graph counter. Then spin the spinner 5 times. Before each spin, ask the students to show you where they think the arrow will land (thumbs up green, thumbs down yellow). Make a record (tallies) of the outcomes on the chalkboard or chart paper.

After five spins, discuss the results. Ask: Did it land on green more times?

Show the students the graph by clicking on the Record Results button. Spin the spinner 20 more times by typing 20 in the Spins box in the lower right-hand corner. Discuss the results.

Model the Activity

Read the Secret Spinner Card that says "Make a spinner that is one-half blue and one-half red" to the class. Ask a student to tell you how to create this virtual spinner on the website. Using the Secret Spinner Record Sheet, model creating the spinner and making predictions for the first four trials. Conduct Trials #1 and #2 using single spins and tally marks. Conduct Trials #3 and #4 using the multiple-spin option. Be sure to model how to spin the spinner multiple times and how to clear the graph between trials. Tell students that they will choose the number of spins for Trials #5, #6, #7, and #8. Point out the two questions at the bottom of the record sheet. Remind students to color the circle to show their spinner.

Model how to create the bar graph from the data collected in Trial #4. Be sure to discuss the scale. Ask: Should each box in the bar be worth 1, 2, or 3? What does the data dictate? Model how to fill in the numbers on the scale on the left side of the graph. Fill in the names of the colors you will be using under the bars. (The Bar Graph Template is designed to be used with many different results. The students will need to decide the increments they should use to create their bar graph. Equal increments should be used. There are 30 spaces in each bar. If the spinner landed on each color 30 or fewer times, students can use increments of one. In this case they would label the *y*-axis from 1 to 30. If the spinner landed on a color more than 30 times, the students will need to use increments of 2 or more. They might label the *y*-axis from 2 to 60 or from 3 to 90.)

Tell students that they will need to color the large spinner template to look like their virtual spinner.

Emphasize that students should keep their spinners secret from the rest of the class. At the end of the activity, students will match the secret spinners to the bar graphs.

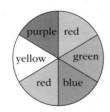

(It is possible to make a virtual spinner with the same color in separate sections, but it is tricky. Suppose you want to make a spinner that looks like this one. On the "Spinner" website, click on Change Spinner. Type "purple, red, green, blue, red, yellow" in the text boxes. To set the colors, put your curser in the box you want to set. Click on the color you want. **Here's the trick: You must set the second red section first.** If you set the first red section first, it will not allow you to set the second section to red. Note: When you use this type of spinner on the website, the graph records the two red sections separately.)

Students Work in Small Groups of 3 or 4

Each group will:

- Find the Secret Spinner Card in their envelope. Follow the directions on the card to create a specific virtual spinner.
- List the possible outcomes of the spinner on their Secret Spinner Record Sheet.
- Predict the outcomes of the first four trials (Trial #1–6 spins, Trial #2–12 spins, Trial #3–60 spins, Trial #4–120 spins).
- Conduct the first four trials by spinning the virtual spinner. Record the results on the Secret Spinner Record Sheet.
- Use the data from Trial #4 to create a bar graph using the Bar Graph Template.
- Use the Spinner Template to create a paper copy of their virtual spinner.
- Conduct Trials #5–8. Students can decide how many times to spin the spinner for each of these trials. They should make a prediction for each experiment before conducting it.
- Draw their spinner on the Secret Spinner Record Sheet.
- Discuss and write an answer to the following questions: How did you choose the number of spins in each trial? Do your experimental results represent your spinner?
- Post their graph in a central location. Give their paper spinner to the teacher.

Follow-Up Discussion

After all the bar graphs have been posted, post the spinners together in a group. Give each student a copy of the Secret Spinner Class Summary Page. Allow 5–10 minutes for students to individually record their predictions on the Secret Spinner Class Summary Page.

Ask students to share their predictions with a partner. Students should discuss the matches they made and justify their decisions to their partner. (When a probability experiment has very few trials, the results can be misleading. The more times an experiment is done [i.e., the spinner is spun], the closer the experimental probability comes to the theoretical probability.)

Lead a whole-group activity to physically match the paper spinners to the bar graphs. Before starting, tell students they are not allowed to match the spinner and bar graph that their group made. Call on one student at a time to chose a spinner and match it to a graph. The student must tell why he/she thinks the spinner matches the graph. Have the other students show a "thumbs up" if they agree. If students disagree, they should tell why. Continue having students match spinners to graphs until all the matches are made.

Student Assessment

- Can the student create a spinner based on given criteria?
- Can the student tell all the possible outcomes that could result from spinning a spinner?
- Does the student accurately record probabilities as fractions?
- Does the student make reasonable predictions? Can the student explain the reasons for his/her predictions?
- Can the student explain why the experimental results represent the spinner or why they do not? Are the student's justifications reasonable?
- Does the student use appropriate vocabulary such as *outcome*, *fraction*, *likely*, *unlikely*, and *chance*?
- Does the bar graph accurately portray the results of the probability experiment?

What to Expect from Students

Sample student work on the activity sheet is shown below.

How did you choose the number of spins each trail?

The number of spins had to be a Multiple of 6. We doubled the number of spins each time.

Draw your spinner. Do your experimental results represent your spinner?

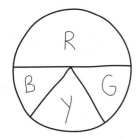

Not exactly, while red was almost always higher than the others, the 3 equal colors were not always equal in the number of spins.

Extensions and Connections

Ask students to design virtual spinners such as the following:

→ A two-color spinner that has a slightly better chance of landing on red
→ A spinner that has a much greater chance of landing on blue than red
→ A spinner that has no chance of spinning red
→ A four-color spinner that has an equal chance for all four colors
→ A four-color spinner that has a much greater chance of getting one of the colors than any other color
→ A spinner that has a $\frac{3}{8}$ probability of getting blue
→ A spinner that is three times more likely to spin green than blue
→ A spinner that has a $\frac{1}{2}$ probability of spinning red and a $\frac{1}{4}$ probability of spinning blue
→ A spinner that has a $\frac{5}{6}$ chance of NOT spinning green
→ A three-color spinner that is twice as likely to spin one color as the other two
→ A spinner that has a $\frac{1}{4}$ chance of spinning blue, a $\frac{1}{8}$ chance of spinning green, and a $\frac{1}{2}$ chance of spinning red
→ A spinner that works like flipping a coin
→ A spinner that works like rolling a die

Have students conduct probability experiments with the spinners and graph the results. Ask: Do your experimental results represent your spinner? Why or why not?

Secret Spinners Record Sheet
Group # _____

List all the possible outcomes for your spinner. For each trial, record your prediction for how many times each outcome will occur. Spin the virtual spinner as many times as the trial calls for. Record the outcomes.

Possible Outcomes	Trial #1 (6 spins)		Trial #2 (12 spins)		Trial #3 (60 spins)		Trial #4 (120 spins)	
	Prediction	Actual	Prediction	Actual	Prediction	Actual	Prediction	Actual

Possible Outcomes	Trial #5 (____ spins)		Trial #6 (____ spins)		Trial #7 (____ spins)		Trial #8 (____ spins)	
	Prediction	Actual	Prediction	Actual	Prediction	Actual	Prediction	Actual

How did you choose the number of spins in each trial?

Draw your spinner. Do your experimental results represent your spinner?

Secret Spinners Activity

Bar Graph Template

Make a bar graph to record your data from Trial #4.

Group # _____

Number of Spins

Color _____ _____ _____ _____ _____ _____

Secret Spinners –
Large Spinner Template

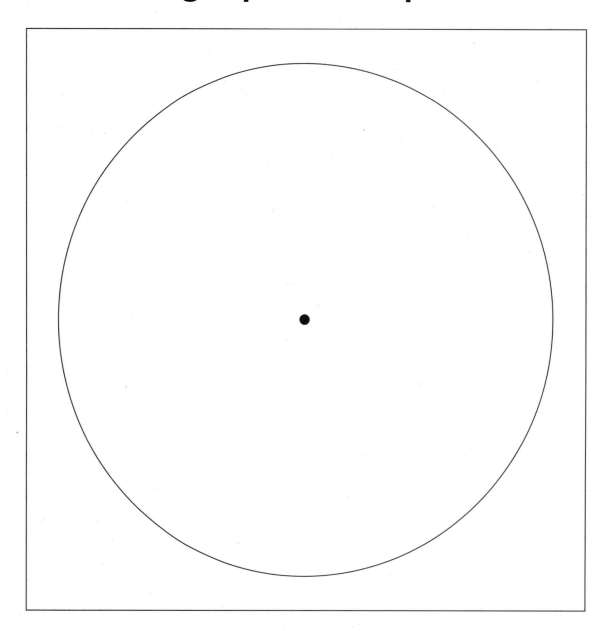

Secret Spinner Cards

Secret Spinners

Go to the National Library of Virtual Manipulatives
http://nlvm.usu.edu/en/nav/vlibrary.html

Click on the box in the matrix:
3–5, Data Analysis & Probability

Click on "Spinners"

Make a spinner that is
one-third green
one-third orange
one-sixth blue
one-sixth red

Secret Spinners

Go to the National Library of Virtual Manipulatives
http://nlvm.usu.edu/en/nav/vlibrary.html

Click on the box in the matrix:
3–5, Data Analysis & Probability

Click on "Spinners"

Make a spinner that is
one-half red
one-sixth green
one-sixth orange
one-sixth blue

Secret Spinners

Go to the National Library of Virtual Manipulatives
http://nlvm.usu.edu/en/nav/vlibrary.html

Click on the box in the matrix:
3–5, Data Analysis & Probability

Click on "Spinners"

Make a spinner that is
five-sixth red
one-sixth blue

Secret Spinners

Go to the National Library of Virtual Manipulatives
http://nlvm.usu.edu/en/nav/vlibrary.html

Click on the box in the matrix:
3–5, Data Analysis & Probability

Click on "Spinners"

Make a spinner that is
two-thirds green
one-sixth blue
one-sixth red

Secret Spinners

Go to the National Library of Virtual Manipulatives
http://nlvm.usu.edu/en/nav/vlibrary.html

Click on the box in the matrix:
3–5, Data Analysis & Probability

Click on "Spinners"

Make a spinner that is
one-half blue
one-sixth yellow
one-sixth red
one-sixth green

Secret Spinners

Go to the National Library of Virtual Manipulatives
http://nlvm.usu.edu/en/nav/vlibrary.html

Click on the box in the matrix:
3–5, Data Analysis & Probability

Click on "Spinners"

Make a spinner that is
one-half red
one-sixth yellow
one-sixth green
one-sixth blue

Secret Spinner Cards

Secret Spinners

Go to the National Library of Virtual Manipulatives
http://nlvm.usu.edu/en/nav/vlibrary.html

Click on the box in the matrix:
3–5, Data Analysis & Probability

Click on "Spinners"

Make a spinner that is
one-third red
one-third blue
one-third green

Secret Spinners

Go to the National Library of Virtual Manipulatives
http://nlvm.usu.edu/en/nav/vlibrary.html

Click on the box in the matrix:
3–5, Data Analysis & Probability

Click on "Spinners"

Make a spinner that is
two-thirds blue
one-sixth red
one-sixth green

Secret Spinners

Go to the National Library of Virtual Manipulatives
http://nlvm.usu.edu/en/nav/vlibrary.html

Click on the box in the matrix:
3–5, Data Analysis & Probability

Click on "Spinners"

Make a spinner that is
one-sixth green   one-sixth yellow
one-sixth orange   one-sixth red
one-sixth purple   one-sixth blue

Secret Spinners

Go to the National Library of Virtual Manipulatives
http://nlvm.usu.edu/en/nav/vlibrary.html

Click on the box in the matrix:
3–5, Data Analysis & Probability

Click on "Spinners"

Make a spinner that is
one-sixth green
one-third red
one-sixth orange
one-third blue

Secret Spinners

Go to the National Library of Virtual Manipulatives
http://nlvm.usu.edu/en/nav/vlibrary.html

Click on the box in the matrix:
3–5, Data Analysis & Probability

Click on "Spinners"

Make a spinner that is
two-thirds red
one-third blue

Secret Spinners

Go to the National Library of Virtual Manipulatives
http://nlvm.usu.edu/en/nav/vlibrary.html

Click on the box in the matrix:
3–5, Data Analysis & Probability

Click on "Spinners"

Make a spinner that is
one-half blue
one-half red

Probability Experiment

Grade-Level Band

6–8

Discussion of the Mathematics

In this lesson, students will develop an understanding of probability by conducting experiments using spinners. Students will analyze the difference between experimental probability and theoretical probability. They should notice that the experimental probability approaches the theoretical probability as the number of spins increases. Students need to have a basic understanding of probability as a fractional part before attempting this investigation.

NCTM Standards

Data Analysis and Probability

- Understand and apply basic concepts of probability
- Develop and evaluate inferences and predictions that are based on data
- Understand and use appropriate terminology to describe complementary and mutually exclusive events
- Use proportionality and a basic understanding of probability to make and test conjectures about the results of experiments and simulations

Lesson Objectives

Upon successful completion of this lesson, the student will be able to:

- Predict the outcomes of simple experiments using spinners and test the predictions
- Determine the probability of a given simple event
- Write probability as ratios and percents
- Identify the difference between theoretical probability and experimental probability
- Describe experimental and expected outcomes

Virtual Manipulatives Websites

National Library of Virtual Manipulatives for Interactive Mathematics: http://nlvm.usu.edu/en/nav/vlibrary.html

Grade Band 6–8, Data Analysis & Probability, Spinners: http://nlvm.usu.edu/en/nav/frames_asid_186_g_3_t_5.html?open=activities

Materials

- A computer with Internet connection for every two students
- "Probability Experiment" activity sheet for each pair of students

Mathematical Vocabulary

theoretical probability, experimental probability, expected outcome, ratio, fraction, percent

Activity and Teacher Notes

Approximate Duration of the Lesson

60 minutes

Model the Activity

Show students how to log on to the *National Library of Virtual Manipulatives* website and find the virtual spinner. (Click on the intersection of *Grade Band 6–8* and *Data Analysis & Probability*. Select the "Spinners" activity.)

There are 5 colors on the spinner: red, yellow, green, purple, and orange. Ask students to predict what the outcome will be for each color on the spinner if you spin the spinner 10 times. Tell them to record the expected outcomes on their activity sheets in fractions and percents.

Show students how to spin the spinner by clicking the Spin button. Model how to record the results of the spins using tally marks. After spinning the spinner a few times, ask students how many times the spinner has landed on red *or* blue. (Use two colors that the spinner has landed on in your results.) Tell students that "or" means that either event occurred so they should add the outcomes together. Ask students how many times the spinner has landed on purple *and* green. "And" means both events occur at the same time. Ask: Is it possible for the spinner to land on two colors at the same time?

Show students how to click on Record Results to display the graph. Clear the graph and type 5 in the box next to Spins. Click Spin to spin the spinner 5 times. Discuss the results shown in the bar graph with students. Ask students to give you a different number to type in the box. Ask students to predict what the graph will look like after you spin the spinner. Spin the spinner and discuss the results. Show students how to clear the results of the graph.

Students Work with Partners
Tell students to log on to the Virtual Library website, complete the three experiments, and answer the questions on the "Probability Experiment" activity sheet.

Teacher Tip
Students may have difficulty thinking proportionally when comparing the three experiments. Using the percentages to compare results will help them understand, for example, that even though red occurred more often in an experiment, proportionally it occurred in a smaller percentage of the spins.

Follow-Up Discussion
After students have completed the activity, bring the class together to discuss their findings.

Student Assessment

- Can the student tell the expected outcomes of an experiment in fractions and percents?
- Can the student compare the expected outcomes and the experimental outcomes?
- Is the student able to describe how the experimental results represent or do not represent the spinner?

- Can the student describe how the experimental outcomes more closely represent the expected outcomes in experiments with more spins?
- Can the student explain the difference between theoretical and experimental probabilities?

What to Expect from Students

- Students may confuse the numerator and denominator when expressing probability as a fraction. Guide students to the understanding that the denominator represents the total possible outcomes, and the numerator represents the desired number of outcomes.
- Students may confuse theoretical and experimental probabilities. They may assume that the experimental probability has to equal the theoretical probability of a given situation.
- Students may begin to see that the more trials that are completed, the closer the experimental probability will get to the theoretical probability.

Extensions and Connections

Have students create their own spinner, predict the results of an experiment with 500 spins, conduct the experiment, and compare the theoretical and experimental probabilities.

Probability Experiment

Vocabulary

Experimental probability is found using frequencies obtained in an experiment or game.

Theoretical probability is the expected probability of an event occurring.

$P(n)$ = number of times the event occurs/number of possible outcomes.

Log on to: http://nlvm.usu.edu/en/nav/vlibrary.html
Click: Virtual Library button
Click: *Data Analysis & Probability* and *6–8*
Click: "Spinners"

Before you begin this experiment, write down what you expect the outcome to be given there are five different colors on the spinner. Use fractions and percents to record your results in the table below.

Color	Expected Outcome		Experimental Outcome		
	Fraction	Percent	Tally	Fraction	Percent
Green					
Red					
Yellow					
Purple					
Orange					

Click the spinner 10 times and then record the results in the table. Answer questions 1–4 using the data in the table above.

1. Using the experimental outcome, what is the probability that you would land on red or green?

    P (red **or** green) =_____

2. Using the experimental outcome, what is the probability that you would land on both yellow and purple?

   P (yellow **and** purple) = _____

3. What is the sum of all the expected outcomes? (Add the expected outcomes column.) _____

4. What is the sum of all the experimental outcomes? (Add the experimental outcomes column.) _____

5. You will repeat the experiment, this time spinning 100 times. Predict the expected outcomes in the table below.

6. Click on Record Results. Clear the graph. Then type 100 in the box next to Spins. Click Spin to spin the spinner 100 times. Read the results in the graph. Record the results of the experiment below.

Color	Expected Outcome		Experimental Outcome	
	Fraction	Percent	Fraction	Percent
Green				
Red				
Yellow				
Purple				
Orange				

7. Does the experimental probability change from your first to your second experiment? How? Why?

   _____

   _____

8. Compare the expected outcome and experimental outcome for each experiment. Did the results change when you spun the spinner more times? How?

   _____

9. Do you think it would it make any difference in the experimental outcome if you spun the spinner 1,000 times? Why or why not?

_____

10. Record the expected outcomes in the table below.

11. Spin the spinner 1,000 times. Record your results.

Color	Expected Outcome		Experimental Outcome	
	Fraction	Percent	Fraction	Percent
Green				
Red				
Yellow				
Purple				
Orange				

12. What did you notice about the last experiment? What happens to the experimental probability as you increase the number of spins in the experiment?

_____

_____

13. Explain in your own words the difference between experimental probability and theoretical probability.

_____

_____

14. <u>Extension</u>: Give a real-life example of how probability can be used. Can probability be used to make decisions? Explain.

_____

_____

Sample Lesson 15:
Data Analysis & Probability

Scatterplots

Grade-Level Band

6–8

Discussion of the Mathematics

In this lesson, students will develop an understanding of scatterplots. Scatterplots are used to examine relationships between two sets of data. To see if two variables are related, you can plot them as ordered pairs on a coordinate grid. This visual representation is called a *scatterplot*. The scatterplot gives us a way to analyze the data for trends or patterns. Sometimes the data points seem to slant in an upward direction, sometimes in a downward direction. Sometimes the data show no particular pattern at all. If the variables are related, the scatterplot will show a linear pattern, approximating a straight line. The stronger the relationship, the closer the data points come to forming a straight line.

When scatterplots have a basic linear pattern, we try to find a *line of best fit*. The line of best fit is the line that comes closest to connecting the points in the scatterplot. It won't pass through all of the points in the scatterplot, but it roughly balances the points that lie above and below it. The line of best fit shows the trend between the two sets of data.

If the line of best fit rises from left to right, it shows a *direct relationship* and has a *positive correlation*. If it falls from left to right, it shows an *inverse relationship* and has a *negative correlation*. *Strong correlations* have data points very close to the line of best fit. *Weak correlations* have data points that are not clustered near the line of best fit. Data points that are not close to the line of best fit are called *outliers*.

Before embarking on this lesson, students should know how to plot points on a coordinate grid. They should know the difference between the *x*-coordinate and the *y*-coordinate of a point and how to name the coordinates of a particular point on the grid.

NCTM Standards

Data Analysis and Probability
- Select, create, and use appropriate graphical representations of data, including scatterplots
- Discuss and understand the correspondence between data sets and their graphical representations, especially scatterplots

Lesson Objectives
Upon successful completion of this lesson, the student will be able to:
- Interpret data sets using scatterplots
- Interpret variables in a scatterplot as having a positive or a negative relationship
- Interpret variables in a scatterplot as having a strong or a weak relationship
- Make inferences, conjectures, and predictions based on analysis of scatterplots

Virtual Manipulatives Websites
National Library of Virtual Manipulatives for Interactive Mathematics: http://nlvm.usu.edu/en/nav/vlibrary.html

Grade Band 6–8, Data Analysis & Probability, Scatterplot: http://nlvm.usu.edu/en/nav/frames_asid_144_g_3_t_5.html?open=activities&from=category_g_3_t_5.html

Materials
- A computer with Internet connection for every two students
- "Scatterplots" activity sheet for each student
- One copy of the information sheet for each student
- One ruler for each pair of students
- A large chart showing sleep/test score data

Mathematical Vocabulary

scatterplot, line of best fit, regression line, trend, pattern, linear, correlation, relationship, positive correlation, negative correlation, strong correlation, weak correlation, direct relationship, inverse relationship, outlier

Activity and Teacher Notes

Preparation

1. Make a chart of the student sleep/test score data (see *Model the Activity*).
2. Copy one Scatterplot Information Sheet for each student.
3. Copy one Scatterplot Activity Sheet for each pair of students.

Approximate Duration of the Lesson

60 minutes

Warm-Up Discussion

Ask students if they think there is a relationship between the amount of sleep they get the night before a test and their test scores. Accept reasonable answers and explanations (e.g., yes, the more rested you are the better you think; yes, if you stay up all night studying, you'll do better; no, it makes no difference).

Model the Activity

Tell students that you asked a group of students how much sleep they got the night before a test, and show a table of the data. Tell students that you're going to create a scatterplot with these two sets of data.

Using an LCD projector and computer with Internet connection, go to the *National Library of Virtual Manipulatives*. Click on the intersection of *Grade Band 6–8* and *Data Analysis & Probability*. Then click on "Scatterplot."

First, set the scale. Leave the minimums at 0. Leave the *x* maximum at 10. Change the *y* maximum to 100. Click Apply. Show the students how to enter the data by clicking on each data point on the grid. Show students how to delete a point if they make a mistake by holding the control key and clicking on the point. (Note: This applet also allows the user to type the data in the *xy* chart; however, this will sometimes change the scale).

Tell students that the line on the graph is the line of best fit and the yellow dot is the point of averages for the data sets.

Student's Name	# Hours of Sleep	Test Score
Victor	7.5	79
Rebecca	8	85
Chris	7.5	92
Temika	7	82
Nathaniel	4	60
Carmen	6	70
Jackson	5	67
Crissie	6.5	85
David	4.5	72
Gerald	6	75
Craig	4.5	73
Hannah	6.5	80
Arielle	6.5	69
Jae-Hyung	7	82
Susie	8	94

Ask students to describe the trend in the data. What is the relationship between sleep and test scores? (The more sleep you get, the better your test score.) Tell students that this is a direct relationship. Statisticians would say that the variables have a positive correlation or a positive relationship.

Ask students to predict the test score of a student who got three hours of sleep the night before the test. What might be a reasonable answer? Why do you think so?

Ask, "How many hours of sleep do you think a student with a test score of 98 got?" Why do you think so?

Give each student a copy of the Scatterplots Information Sheet. Read and discuss the data together. Ask questions such as:

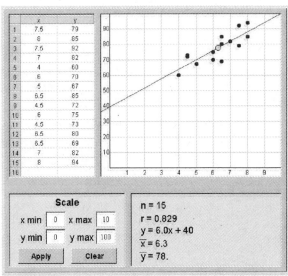

- What does each dot on the scatterplot represent?
- What variable is plotted on the x-axis? The y-axis?
- How can you describe the relationship between sleep and test scores? Why do you think there is a direct relationship?

- What is the relationship between the number of DVD buyers and the cost of the DVD? Why do you think there is an inverse relationship?
- What kind of relationship do temperature and land mass have?
- How can you describe the general trend of the data in the _____ scatterplot?
- How can you tell if a relationship is strong? Weak?
- Why might the relationship between hockey goalies' weight and height be weak? (They all are about the same size. If you had data from people with a larger range of heights, you would see a strong positive relationship between height and weight.)
- Do you see any outliers in the scatterplots on this page?

Students Work with Partners

Put students into groups of two. Give each set of partners a Scatterplots Activity Sheet. Tell the students that they will be creating scatterplots using the virtual scatterplot. Have students read and follow the directions on the activity sheet.

As students work, circulate and observe. Provide assistance when necessary.

Follow-Up Discussion

After students have completed the activity, discuss their findings in a class meeting. First discuss the scatterplots created from the three data sets. Ask questions such as:

- Which of the data sets had direct (positive) relationships? (number of chirps/temperature and age/allowance)
- Was the relationship strong or weak?
- Were there any outliers?
- Based on the data in the scatterplot, how much allowance do you think you should receive? Why?
- Which of the data sets had an inverse (negative) relationship? (study time/socializing time) Why do you think that occurred?
- How can you use a scatterplot to make a prediction?

Have students use the virtual scatterplot to share some of the scatterplots they created. Compare and contrast the scatterplots. (It might be helpful to have students share their drawings so you can look at a few scatterplots at one time.)

- What is the same about all the positive relationships? What is different about them?
- What is the same about all the negative relationships? What is different about them?
- What is the same about all the strong relationships? What is different about them?
- What is the same about all the weak relationships? What is different about them?

Discuss the outlier. What happened to the line of best fit when you added an outlier to your data? What does that tell you about outliers?

After the whole-group discussion, give students a few minutes to read and revise their answer to the last question on the activity sheet (i.e., What have you learned about scatterplots from this lesson?). Have a few students share their thoughts to close the lesson.

Student Assessment

- Can the student describe the general trend of a scatterplot?
- Can the student identify scatterplots showing positive and negative relationships?
- Can the student identify scatterplots showing strong and weak relationships?
- Can the student accurately make a prediction using a scatterplot?
- Does the student use appropriate vocabulary when describing scatterplots?

What to Expect from Students
A sample of student work is shown below (Figure 1).

Extensions and Connections
Have students collect and represent data using virtual scatterplots. Ask students to analyze the data for relationships. Possible data sets that might show relationships include:

- Height and hand span
- Height and weight
- Height and age
- Age and shoe size
- Age and grade level
- Ages of husbands and wives

- Length of stride and number of strides taken in a 100-meter sprint
- The time it takes to run 400 meters and the speed of the runner

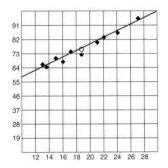

1. Do you notice a relationship between the temperature and the number of chirps? If so, what is it? Is the relationship positive or negative? Is the relationship strong or weak? How do you know?

   The higher the temperature, the more chirps. It is a positive relationship. It is strong because the dots are very close to the line.

2. Make a prediction. If you heard a cricket chirp 18 times in 7 seconds, what might the temperature be? Explain your reasoning.

   It would be about 71 degrees. That is where the line of best fit crosses 18. (18, 71)

3. Make a prediction. If it is 90°F outside, how many cricket chirps would you expect to hear in 7 seconds? Explain your reasoning.

   23 chirps (23, 90) is where the line of best fit crosses 90.

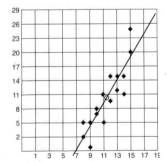

1. Describe the relationship between age and allowance.

   The older you are, the more allowance you get.

2. Are there any outliers in the data? If so, describe them.

   Yes. (15, 25) is an outlier. It is far away from the line of best fit.

3. Based on the data you collected, how much allowance do you think you should be receiving each week? Why?

   I think I should get $14 a week because I am 13 years old. If you start at age 13 and go up to the line of best fit, it crosses at $14.

FIGURE 1. *Sample of student work*

1. Do you notice a relationship between time spent studying and time spent socializing? If so, describe the relationship. Is the relationship positive or negative? Is the relationship strong or weak? How do you know?

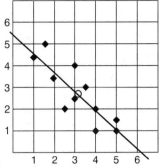

The more you study, the less you socialize. It is negative and not very strong. The points are far away from the line of best fit.

2. Based on the information you collected, do you think you should change your study habits? Why?

No. (2, 3) is pretty close to the line of best fit.

3. If someone told you they studied about 3 hours per day, about how much time would you think they spent socializing? Why?

About 3 hours because (3, 2.9) is on the line of best fit.

4. If someone told you they spent 2.5 hours a day socializing, about how much time would you think they spent studying? Why?

About 3.5 hours because (3.5, 2.5) is on the line of best fit.

1. Create a scatterplot showing a strong positive relationship. Draw your scatterplot below.

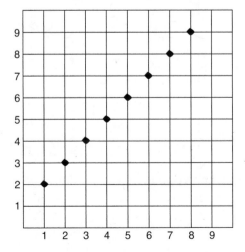

2. Create a scatterplot showing a weak positive relationship. Draw your scatterplot below.

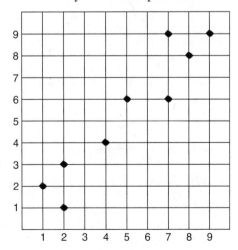

FIGURE I (cont). *Sample of student work*

3. Create a scatterplot showing a strong negative relationship. Draw your scatterplot below.

4. Create a scatterplot showing a weak negative relationship. Draw your scatterplot below.

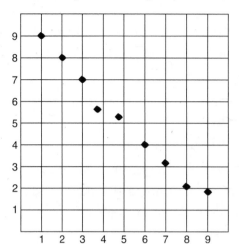 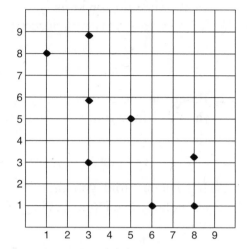

5. Create a scatterplot showing a strong relationship. (It can be either positive or negative.) Draw your scatterplot below. Include the line of best fit in your drawing.

Add an outlier to your scatterplot. Draw the result below. Include the line of best fit in your drawing.

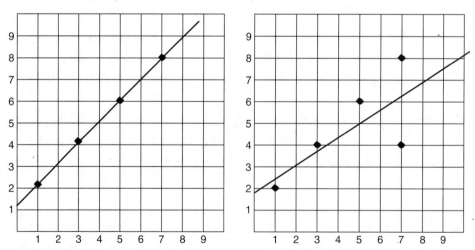

What happened to the line of best fit when you added the outlier to your data?

It moved toward the outlier. It is still positive. It is not as strong.

FIGURE 1 (cont). *Sample of student work*

Scatterplots Information Sheet

What is a scatterplot?

In order to see if two variables are related, you can plot them as ordered pairs on a coordinate grid. This visual representation is called a *scatterplot*. Relationships between variables can be positive or negative, or there may be no relationship at all.

Examples of scatterplots:

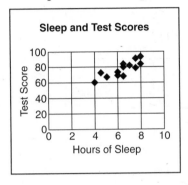

Positive Relationship

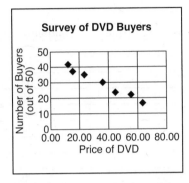

Negative Relationship

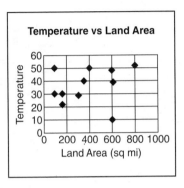

No Relationship

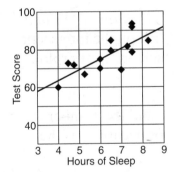

What is a line of best fit?

The line of best fit describes the general trend of the data. It follows the same upward or downward pattern as the data points. It balances out the points that lie above and below the line.

How strong is the relationship?

Strong relationships have data points very close to the line of best fit. Weak relationships have data points that are not clustered near the line of best fit.

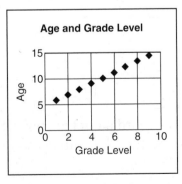

Strong Relationship

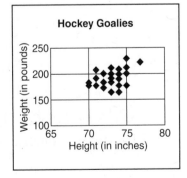

Weak Relationship

What is an outlier?

Data points that are not close to the line of best fit are called *outliers*.

Scatterplots Activity

Scatterplots Activity Sheet

A. Every spring while sitting on your back deck, you hear crickets chirping in the woods. You notice that sometimes the crickets seem to chirp fast and other times the crickets seem to chirp slow. You've heard that the rate of cricket chirps is related to the temperature. You decide to collect some data to see if you can find a relationship. Over the next few weeks, you collect the following data:

# Chirps in 7 Seconds	Temperature (°F)
15	70
16	68
13	63
19	76
22	83
17	74
13	65
27	95
24	86
21	80

Using a computer with Internet connection, go to the *National Library of Virtual Manipulatives* (http://nlvm.usu.edu/en/nav/vlibrary.html). Click on the intersection of *Grade Band 6–8* and *Data Analysis & Probability*. Then click on" Scatterplot." Enter your cricket data into the scatterplot grid.

1. Do you notice a relationship between the temperature and the number of chirps? If so, what is it? Is the relationship positive or negative? Is the relationship strong or weak? How do you know?

2. Make a prediction. If you heard a cricket chirp 18 times in 7 seconds, what might the temperature be? Explain your reasoning.

3. Make a prediction. If it is 90°F outside, how many cricket chirps would you expect to hear in 7 seconds? Explain your reasoning.

B. Your parents give you $5.00 a week for allowance. You don't think that's enough for someone your age. You poll your friends to see how much allowance they get, hoping to be able to make an argument to your parents for more money. Enter the following data in the virtual scatterplot.

Age	Weekly Allowance (in dollars)
8	2
15	25
8	5
14	15
13	15
9	5
13	12
12	15

Age	Weekly Allowance (in dollars)
15	20
9	0
14	11
11	5
10	7
10	8
12	10
11	10

1. Describe the relationship between age and allowance.

2. Are there any outliers in the data? If so, describe them.

3. Based on the data you collected, how much allowance do you think you should be receiving each week? Why?

Name _____ Date _____

C. You study 2 hours every night, and you get good grades. You still have time to hang out with your friends after school for about 3 hours every afternoon. You'd like to have more time to socialize with your friends, but you wonder if this would leave you less time to study. You decide to poll your friends to see how much time they spend studying and socializing. Analyze the following data using the virtual scatterplot.

Name	Study (hrs per day)	Socialize (hrs per day)
Chris	2	3.5
C.J.	5	1
Jillian	4	2
Sharon	1.5	5
Temika	5	1.5
Jane	3.5	3
Carlos	3	2.5
Mahad	4	1
Natasha	2.5	2
Kayla	3	4
Aaron	1	4.5

1. Do you notice a relationship between time spent studying and time spent socializing? If so, describe the relationship. Is the relationship positive or negative? Is the relationship strong or weak? How do you know?

2. Based on the information you collected, do you think you should change your study habits? Why?

3. If someone told you he studied about 3 hours per day, about how much time would you think he spent socializing? Why?

Scatterplots Activity (page 4)

4. If someone told you she spent 2.5 hours a day socializing, about how much time would you think she spent studying? Why?

D. Clear the virtual scatterplot.
Set the scale as the picture shows.
Click Apply.

Create the following scatterplots.
Remember to click Clear before creating each new scatterplot.

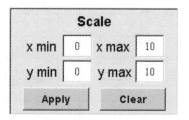

1. Create a scatterplot showing a strong positive relationship. Draw your scatterplot below.

2. Create a scatterplot showing a weak positive relationship. Draw your scatterplot below.

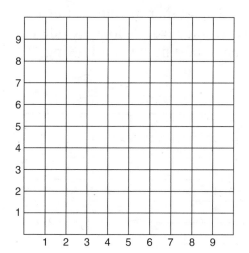

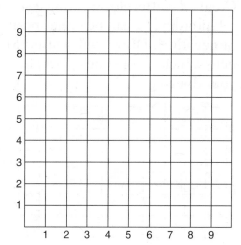

Name _____   Date _____

3. Create a scatterplot showing a strong negative relationship. Draw your scatterplot below.

4. Create a scatterplot showing a weak negative relationship. Draw your scatterplot below.

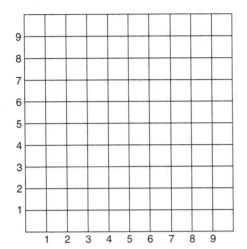

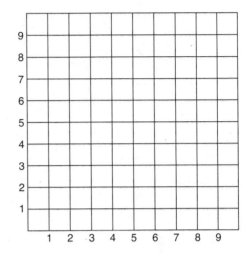

5. Create a scatterplot showing a strong relationship. (It can be either positive or negative.) Draw your scatterplot below. Include the line of best fit in your drawing.

Add an outlier to your scatterplot. Draw the result below. Include the line of best fit in your drawing.

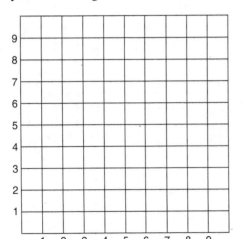

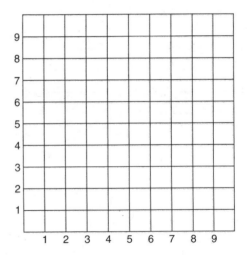

What happened to the line of best fit when you added the outlier to your data?

Scatterplots Activity (page 6)

6. What have you learned about scatterplots from this lesson?